EARLY GREEK LAW

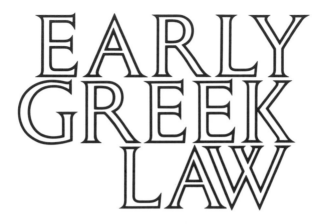

EARLY GREEK LAW

MICHAEL GAGARIN

UNIVERSITY OF CALIFORNIA PRESS
Berkeley   Los Angeles   London

K
281
G262
1986

LC

University of California Press
Berkeley and Los Angeles, California
University of California Press, Ltd. London, England

© 1986 by The Regents of the University of California

Library of Congress Cataloging-in-Publication Data
Gagarin, Michael.
Early Greek law.
Bibliography: p.
1. Law, Greek. I. Title.
LAW   340.5'3'8   85-28816
ISBN 0-520-05678-7 (alk. paper)

Printed in the United States of America
1 2 3 4 5 6 7 8 9

5-5-87

FOR DANIEL

CONTENTS

PREFACE

The following study owes more than I can express to the help and guidance of others. I have tried to acknowledge their published work in my notes, though I have frequently, I am sure, failed to cite every source for an idea. The bibliography contains only those items referred to in the notes, although numerous other works not cited, especially of legal history and anthropology, have influenced my thinking.

The work was read in an earlier version by Eric Havelock, Martin Ostwald, and Ronald Stroud. Alan Boegehold and Douglas MacDowell read the book for the University of California Press and made a number of helpful suggestions. At the final stage Mogens Hansen gave the work an extensive and thoughtful critique. I am grateful to all these scholars for their helpful advice and criticism. The work benefited greatly from two careful readings by Dr. Mark Damen, whose assigned task was to check the accuracy of citations, Greek quotations, and so forth, but who also helped me clarify both my writing and my thinking at numerous points. I also thank the staff of the University of California Press, especially Doris Kretschmer and Mary Lamprech, for their friendly and helpful treatment of the work.

The main work on this book was completed during 1980–81, while I held a Research Fellowship from the American Council of Learned Societies supplemented by a grant from the University Research Institute of the University of Texas. I gratefully acknowledge the assistance of these grants, without which I could never have undertaken a project such as this.

Finally, I dedicate the book to my son, Daniel, whose infant presence during that year not only provided a refreshing contrast to the rarefied atmosphere of my library study, but also inspired me to frequent reflection on the nature of human beings and the need for order in human society.

1

INTRODUCTION:
LAW IN HUMAN
SOCIETY

The recognition that law is a basic feature of human society distinguishing men from animals is at least as old as the Greek poet Hesiod, who says in the *Works and Days* (lines 276–80): "Zeus established the following way of life [*nomos*] for men: whereas for fish and beasts and winged birds it is the custom to eat one another, since there is no law [*dikē*] among them, to men he gave law, which is by far the best thing."[1] In the following chapters I shall explore how law came into existence in ancient Greece, where the rule of law was one of the most important creations of the newly developing polis, or city-state. Before examining the emergence of law during the archaic period, however, it may be helpful to clarify what I mean by "law." The following remarks are not intended to serve as a general introduction to legal theory or legal anthropology.[2] They are simply an attempt to clarify my own thinking on certain issues that will arise in subsequent chapters.

In seeking to delineate precisely the boundaries of law in a society, we may begin with the useful (if superficial) division between rules, which make up the social order, and procedures, which serve to redress violations of those rules or which in general help settle

1. For *dikē* in the sense of "law" see Gagarin 1973 and the end of chap. 2 below. For *nomos* as "way of life" in this passage see Ostwald 1969, 21; cf. West 1978, ad loc. Shipp has recently argued that the basic sense of *nomos* in Greek (and in this passage) is "law" rather than "custom": "Hesiod uses *nomos* of divine ordinance as a primitive anticipation of scientific 'law' of nature" (Shipp 1978, 11). This view, like much of Shipp's argument, is vitiated by a failure to distinguish between different English senses of "law."

2. The best recent work on legal theory is Hart 1961. For a good introduction to the anthropology of law, see Roberts 1979; for a brief survey of anthropological work on law, see Humphreys 1985a.

disputes. In traditional terms these are substantive and procedural law.[3] A double question then arises: On the one hand, among all the rules of a society, from social customs or rules of etiquette to formal written statutes, how do we determine which are substantive laws? On the other hand, among all the means of enforcing rules, from a sense of guilt or the disapproval of friends to punishment by a modern judicial system, and among all the various means of settling disputes, from informal agreement or arbitration by family and friends to formal court action, how do we determine which are *legal* procedures?

Most theoretical discussion has centered on the question concerning rules, and recently the most influential and, to my mind, persuasive answer has been given by H. L. A. Hart,[4] who distinguishes between "primary rules," which impose obligations, and "secondary rules," which regulate the creation and operation of the primary rules. The most important secondary rules are "rules of recognition," which tell us how to "recognize" the primary rules— that is, how to know which of a society's rules are laws. Hart's solution works well for a modern literate society such as our own.[5] When we try to apply it to preliterate societies, however, we encounter considerable difficulty, since these appear to lack any clear or explicit means for recognizing laws. As Hart says, writing plays a crucial role in the transition "from the pre-legal to the legal."[6]

3. On the distinction between substantive and procedural law see chap. 3 below.
4. Hart 1961, esp. 89–96.
5. Even if one emphasizes, with the "legal realists," the importance of judicial decisions in Anglo-American law (see n. 15 below), one must admit that these decisions are based at least to some extent on formally expressed (i.e., "recognized") law in the form of either written statutes or previous court decisions. Dworkin (1977) objects that judges and juries are influenced by principles; they are also influenced by irrational prejudices, by religious and moral precepts, by social customs and attitudes, etc. But it serves no useful purpose to treat these as laws, unless or until they are formally recognized either by statute or by the explicit statement of an authoritative body such as a court. Much of what Dworkin says about the importance of general principles may be true, but none of it really damages Hart's position. See Mandel 1979 and Hart 1983, 6–8, 123–44.
6. Hart 1961, 92. More recently, Schlegel (1970, 152–64) has argued for a rule of recognition among the nonliterate Tiruray of the Philippines; on this point, however, he has seriously misunderstood Hart, and his rule of recognition turns out to be only the most general moral principle of the Tiruray (roughly, "do not hurt the feelings of others"), which, as Schlegel acknowledges, does not serve to differentiate legal rules from moral rules.

It may seem arbitrary to restrict the term "law" to societies with written statutes, and many anthropologists and other scholars, perhaps unhappy with the implication that primitive societies might have no law, have wished to use the term to designate at least some aspects of preliterate societies. The question remains, however, how does one distinguish laws from all the other rules in these societies?

One approach, exemplified by Malinowski, is to treat as laws those rules in a preliterate society that cover the same areas of behavior as our own laws.[7] Many anthropologists, however, have rejected this approach as a misrepresentation of the nature of these rules.[8] Malinowski certainly demonstrates the existence of regular, purposeful patterns of, for example, gift-exchange among various segments of Trobriand society, but to designate these customary practices as a kind of commercial law is in the view of many scholars a distortion.

Instead of looking for rules corresponding to our laws, many anthropologists have resorted to the idea of the enforcement of rules by society. Thus Radcliffe-Brown writes that "the field of law will therefore be regarded as coterminous with that of organized legal sanctions,"[9] and Schapera argues that although "the Tswana have no written or even oral codes setting aside legal rules from all others," nonetheless "the rules of conduct distinguished from the rest by the ultimate sanction of judicial enforcement may for all practical purposes be regarded as the 'laws' of the Tswana."[10] A broader, but essentially similar statement of this view is Hoebel's famous definition: "A social norm is legal if its neglect or infraction is regularly met, in threat or in fact, by the application of physical force by an individual or group possessing the socially recognized privilege of so acting."[11]

The basic approach exemplified by these views is to define legal rules in a preliterate society in terms of sanctions and procedures established in order to redress violations of those rules. This ap-

7. Malinowski: "There exists a class of binding rules which control most aspects of tribal life, which regulate personal relations between kinsmen, clansmen and tribesmen, settle economic relations, the exercise of power and of magic, the status of husband and wife and of their respective families. These are the rules of a Melanesian community which correspond to our civil law" (1926, 66).
8. See Seagle 1937, esp. 282–85, and more generally Seagle 1941, 33–34.
9. Radcliffe-Brown 1933a, 202.
10. Schapera 1970, 35–37.
11. Hoebel 1954, 28.

proach seems to work well for certain kinds of rules in certain societies, but it contains several assumptions that must be more closely examined: that there exist sanctions in all societies with law, that we can define certain procedures as legal, and that disputes which arise in preliterate societies can normally be analyzed in terms of a rule and its violation.

To take the last of these assumptions first (I shall return to the first two points later), it is apparent from anthropological reports of tribal societies that not all disputes involve the clear violation of a rule. Sometimes two or more rules, or no rule, may apply to a given situation, or disputes may arise simply because the legitimate claims or courses of action of two parties come into conflict.[12] To illustrate this consider a case from the Arusha of northern Tanzania.[13] Briefly summarized, the dispute concerns a piece of land in between two men's fields. Ownership of the land had long been disputed and it remained uncultivated until one of the men, without notice, hoed up and planted for himself a narrow strip of this disputed land. The other man brought the matter to the parish assembly, whence it was referred to a local moot. The moot agreed that the defendant had acted imprudently in hoeing up the disputed strip, but he was allowed to retain the piece of land, since the plaintiff had a considerable amount of land for himself whereas the defendant had little. The plaintiff had also lost much of his support in the community by the overly aggressive way in which he had brought the case and by his unwillingness to be generous to his more needy neighbor.

One could say that this case concerns the violation of a rule, perhaps the rule that one should not cultivate land not clearly one's own, but such an analysis would be inadequate. In the final settlement the defendant's apparent violation of this rule is ignored in favor of other rules, such as that one should be generous toward a needy neighbor, or that one should be restrained in pursuing disputes about relatively small matters. Rather, the case concerns the application of a number of different and conflicting rules to a given situation, and it cannot be analyzed by the simple model of a rule violation. There are legitimate claims on both sides, and the court

12. Cf. the distinction drawn by Comaroff and Roberts (1981, esp. 234–42) between cases which involve an action over a specific value (their types 1 and 2) and cases which concern the nature of a relationship (their types 3 and 4).

13. See Gulliver 1963, 190–91. Another good illustration of this point is the case discussed by Roberts 1979, 125–28.

determines not simply whether a rule has been violated but what will be a fair and acceptable resolution of the conflict in the light of several different rules.[14] Thus to the extent that an analysis of law in society focuses only on violations of rules, it is inadequate.

A similar objection is suggested by the legal realists, and more recently Dworkin, in their discussions of modern American law. The realists, for whom judicial decisions are the essence of a legal system,[15] see law as a flexible, unstable process for settling disputes within a context of continually changing and often unpredictable rules. Dworkin's challenge to Hart's positivist analysis is based on the assumption (which seems valid) that many actual cases are decided on the basis of rules or principles other than formal, statutory laws. He argues that one should not exclude these other rules from one's definition of law.[16] Dworkin's challenge does not, in my view, invalidate Hart's analysis of modern law,[17] but a similar challenge can more validly be brought with regard to rules in a preliterate society, where the clear differentiation of laws from other rules does not seem possible, especially in cases involving more than a simple violation of a single clear rule. When many rules enter into the

14. Cf. van Velsen's "situational analysis":

> One of the assumptions on which situational analysis rests is that the norms of society do not constitute a consistent and coherent whole. On the contrary, they are often vaguely formulated and discrepant. It is this fact which allows for their manipulation by members of a society in furthering their own aims, without necessarily impairing its apparently enduring structure of social relationships. . . . Descriptions of "primitive law" frequently imply that all disputes are simple cases of "breaking the law" and that argument therefore is concerned with the "facts" of the case while there is tacit or express agreement among all parties concerned as to the applicable norm or norms. This ignores the point that in any society one is likely to find a large category of disputes where argument is mainly concerned with the question of which of a number of mutually conflicting norms should be applied to the undisputed "facts" of the case. (1967, 146–47)

See also Hart's discussion of clear cases vs. indeterminate rules (1967, 270–71), and cf. Comaroff and Roberts, who describe *mekgwa le melao* (loosely translated as "Tswana law and custom") as comprising "a loosely ordered and undifferentiated repertoire of norms, the substantive content of which varies widely in its nature, value, and specificity" (1981, 70).

15. E.g., Frank: "For any particular lay person, the law, with respect to any particular set of facts, is a decision of a court with respect to those facts so far as that decision affects that particular person" (1930, 46).

16. Dworkin 1977.

17. See n. 5 above.

settlement of a case, it is arbitrary to designate only some of these as laws.

Several points in the preceding discussion suggest that legal rules might be most easily defined in terms of legal procedures. Turning from rules to procedures, however, we find similar difficulties in designating certain procedures as legal. The attempt to define legal procedures in terms of force or sanctions, for example, raises the question, When does a sanction become legal as opposed to simply private? This question is particularly important in discussing the idea of vengeance, a strong force in many preliterate societies. A definition of legal sanctions as those that "are imposed by a constituted authority, political, military or ecclesiastic"[18] simply begs the question. Furthermore, many settlements in preliterate societies are compromises which do not require strongly coercive enforcement. Indeed, some preliterate societies have few, if any, formal means of enforcing settlements, and yet disputes in these societies may be settled with the help of recognized social authorities.[19]

If one specifies, however, that law exists in and must therefore be a part of a particular society,[20] then it may be unnecessary to speak of enforcement. If there is no specific social authority to enforce settlements, then disputes must be settled in a way ultimately acceptable to both parties. Mutually acceptable settlements are found among preliterate people,[21] and as we shall see in the next chapter,

18. Radcliffe-Brown 1933b, 532.
19. Cf. Bryce on early Iceland: "Law in fact existed without any public responsibility for enforcing it, the sanction, on which modern jurists so often dwell as being vital to the conception of law, being found partly in public opinion, partly in the greater insecurity which attached to the life of the person who disregarded a judgement. Yet law was by no means ineffective" (1901, 281). Bryce notes that most decisions were unanimous, or nearly so, and this may have given them more authority; nonetheless, there were still many cases where one party did not accept the settlement and violence broke out.
20. See Nader 1969, 8–10. Other anthropologists have recently talked about the existence of law in smaller subgroups or "corporations" within society. This is an interesting approach, but it seems to me worth preserving the idea that a special kind of law exists for a society as a whole, even though among primitive people it may be difficult to define precisely the boundaries of a society. See Moore 1978, 82–134 (originally published in 1972), whose view is discussed approvingly by Gluckman 1974, 326–33.
21. See, for example, Reid: "For the Cherokee, a legal system functioned successfully if it maintained social harmony through mutual submission to customary procedures exercised by clearly defined groups, such as the clans. There was no need

they seem to be the rule in early Greece. If, on the other hand, a society has developed at least some ability to enforce settlements, then disputes can be settled in a way not acceptable to one party. Even then, however, every society will fall short of complete enforcement. In archaic Greece, as we shall see, enforcement of settlements was a frequent concern of lawgivers. But to whatever degree a society is able to enforce settlements of disputes, it must be the case that most disputes are in fact settled, or at least contained; otherwise the society could not endure.[22]

Since the idea of enforcement does not seem to provide an adequate basis for the definition of legal procedure, let us try a different approach and begin instead with the idea of disputes in the most general sense, whether arising out of the clear violation of a rule or from a more complex conflict of various rules and interests. A dispute requires the involvement of at least two parties. If the dispute is settled, the settlement is brought about by either peaceful or forcible means.[23] Among the various procedures for settling disputes peacefully, I would designate as legal those which have two characteristics. First, they are public, in that they are available to all full members of the community and are generally recognized as being available. In a public procedure the community has normally recognized one or more persons or groups as having a special authority in settling disputes, though not necessarily in enforcing those settlements. Second, legal procedures are formal—not necessarily as formal as the proceedings of a modern court, of course, but at least in the sense of adhering to certain accepted traditions concerning the time, place, and general procedures for presenting a case and arriv-

---

to produce that harmony by coerced submission to sovereign authority channelled through judicial institutions" (1970, 231). See also p. 23, n. 12 below.

22. It is for these reasons that I would hesitate to call "international law" law in the full sense, since the idea of an enduring society of nations is at best a weak one. In certain areas, such as international trade, most disputes are settled by means of accepted rules and procedures, and a society of nations might be said to endure. But in political and military matters it is not yet possible to speak of an enduring international order. Some disputes between parties are settled and certain rules are widely accepted, but other disputes, particularly among the more powerful nations, resist settlement and on many important matters rules either cannot be agreed on or are regularly violated. Thus, if we use the term "international law," we should recognize that at present it is law only in an incomplete sense.

23. Among forceful means I include the threat of force, if this is the primary factor inducing one or both parties to accept a settlement.

ing at a settlement. Thus we may define a legal procedure as a public, formal procedure for peacefully settling disputes between members of a society,[24] and on this definition we may point to legal procedures in many, though not all, preliterate societies.

This analysis suggests a three-stage model for the development of law in society. The first, which I shall call the "pre-legal" stage (though I would not insist on this terminology), is where the society has no recognized (i.e., formal and public) procedures for peacefully settling disputes among its members. I assume that every human society has some means of settling disputes or it could not remain together as a society, but it is possible that in a small group these may be only informal.[25] Many preliterate societies, however, have recognizable procedures for settling disputes that meet the criteria I have set forth, and I shall designate this second stage of development, in which a society has legal procedures but no recognized legal rules (in Hart's sense), as "proto-legal." The third, fully "legal" stage of development is where a society has recognized legal

24. I am aware that there may be gray areas where it is hard to decide whether a procedure is formal or public enough to meet this definition, and anthropologists seem to prefer not to make the distinction at all but rather to see formal and informal, public and private procedures as part of one continuum. But consider hierarchical orderings of procedures, such as that proposed by Comaroff and Roberts (1981, 108), where disputants (1) first try to negotiate between themselves, (2) then ask their families for help, (3) then go to the ward headman, and (4) finally go to the tribal chief. We can see the step from (2) to (3) as a fairly clear transition from private to public procedures, even though this distinction may not be so rigid among the Tswana as it is in a modern society. Similarly in the three-part system described by Whitelam for pre-monarchical Israel, we may draw the line between "family law under the jurisdiction of the *paterfamilias*" and "the adjudication of clan or town disputes by a council of elders or town assembly" (Whitelam 1979, 46). Roberts (1979, 69–78) surveys a whole spectrum of "settlement directed talking" from bilateral negotiation to third-party adjudication.

25. Cf. Evans-Pritchard's famous conclusion: "In a strict sense Nuer have no law." He elaborates, "I lived in intimacy for a year with Nuer and never heard a case brought before an individual or a tribunal of any kind, and, furthermore, I reached the conclusion that it is very rare for a man to obtain redress except by force or threat of force" (1940, 162). But the chief and the elders were apparently sometimes involved in the settlement of disputes (ibid, 163–64) and may perhaps be seen as constituting an informal public institution for dispute settlement. Another group that seems even further removed from law as I have defined it are the Tasaday of the Philippines. The twenty-five or so members of this extremely primitive, cave-dwelling group appear not even to have any disputes among themselves and thus, evidently, they have no means of settling disputes (see Nance 1975).

rules, as well as procedures, a step that almost always requires the knowledge of writing. I would certainly not insist on the universal validity of this or any other model. I claim only that it is a possible model for development, and I believe it will provide a useful framework for examining the emergence of law in early Greece in the following chapters.

Although it is possible at the second, proto-legal, stage to isolate certain rules of behavior that are subject to legal procedures and call them laws,[26] there are two main drawbacks to such a procedure. First, it obscures the important difference between societies that explicitly recognize a group of laws as a special authoritative class, separate from other rules, and those that do not. Second, as we have seen, without some means of formally "recognizing" certain rules as laws it is often difficult or impossible to distinguish between those rules that are subject to legal procedures and those that are not. Thus I find it more useful for the purpose of this study to reserve the term "law" in the strict sense[27] for those rules recognized by the society itself as forming a separate category.[28]

I have spoken about writing as the means of recognizing substantive laws, but it is at least theoretically possible that a society may have an official oral record of its laws preserved by recognized authorities, which would be invoked only or primarily in the settlement of disputes and would have a special authority different from that of other rules in the society.[29] There has been some speculation,

26. This was the standard practice in colonial areas where handbooks listing "the laws" of the native peoples were commonly compiled for use by colonial administrators (e.g., Howell 1954).

27. In general I tend to agree with Gluckman (1965b, 182) that "there is no 'strict sense' of the word 'law.'" We may, nonetheless, employ the word in a strict sense for our present purposes without being dogmatic about an absolute sense of the term.

28. Even when a preliterate society has an expression translatable as "law," their rules do not necessarily have the same status as our own body of law; see, e.g., Comaroff and Roberts on *mekgwa le melao* ("Tswana law and custom," see n. 14 above): "The norms that compose it are seen also to provide criteria and standards that may be invoked in dispute settlement, but they do not constitute a segregated set, distinguished for jural purposes from other kinds of norm and corresponding to 'rules of law' in the sense understood in Western jurisprudence" (1981, 28). See further Roberts 1979, 25–26, 193–94.

29. The idea that among preliterate people a certain person or group was the repository of "customary law" in oral form is as old as Maine (1861, 7); its popularity has not been diminished by the scarcity of actual examples of oral codes.

for example, that early Irish bards memorized and recited collections of laws, though the evidence for this is hardly conclusive.[30] The evidence for "oral laws" in preliterate Iceland is stronger.[31] From the early tenth century until after laws were first written down in 1117–1118 the highest public official in Iceland was the "lawspeaker," who was the sole authority for the text of the country's laws. Among his duties was an annual recitation of one-third of the laws, the complete collection being recited during his three-year term of office. He also had to be available to anyone who wanted to ascertain the law pertaining to any given matter. We do not know the precise text of any of these orally preserved "laws," though most of them seem to have concerned formal procedural matters. It is also difficult to tell just how much authority the lawspeaker had, since the judicial system, which existed in a complex form comprising local and regional bodies from the time of the earliest settlement, did not prevent the frequent resort to extralegal self-help. Such self-help continued to be common until well after the writing down of laws.[32]

With these possible exceptions, laws are recognized primarily by means of writing in all other societies, and certainly in ancient Greece. True, Homer and Hesiod became authoritative texts for the Greeks in oral form, and we do find a few explicit rules of behavior

30. Binchy (1943, 205–7) discusses certain apparent remnants of oral features in early Irish laws preserved in writing.

31. There is a good summary of the Icelandic system in the chapter on "Primitive Iceland" in Bryce 1901, 263–300. For further details see Gjerset 1924, 29–48, Jóhannesson 1974, 35–93, and Hastrup 1985, 205–22.

32. Despite the elaborate judicial system in early Iceland, the traditional code of personal vengeance always remained strong in this period, and the courts were often notably ineffective. As Gjerset puts it:

> With a highly developed jurisprudence and a well organized system of courts they nevertheless failed to maintain social order and to administer justice with efficient impartiality. In the public mind the law lacked majesty and authority. It was regarded as something for lawyers to sharpen their wits upon; something to be evaded, or even ignored. Civic life was not regulated according to the principles of law, but continued to be controlled by custom. (1924, 46)

The early Icelandic sagas (particularly *Njal's Saga*) portray a society in which the widespread use of force often leads to long-lasting vendettas. Legal rules, which seem to consist primarily of rather technical procedural requirements, seldom affect a dispute. I can find no evidence, by the way, that any of the early Icelandic "laws" was in verse. The earliest written texts do not display evidence of oral transmission; see Foote 1977.

in them. But these rules concern a broad range of human behavior, and none of them is singled out as having a special status, not even those rules that we might be tempted to call laws.

Take, for example, Ajax's plea to Achilles in Book 9 of the *Iliad* (632–36): "A man accepts blood-money even for a slain brother or child; and the killer remains in the country, having paid a large sum, and the man's anger and valiant spirit are calmed when he has received the blood-money." Should we call this a law? Certainly it concerns an area of behavior often governed by law in later societies, but it is not cast in the form of a law, namely a general prescription, but is presented as an observation of normal behavior (though, to be sure, it is intended to have prescriptive force). In its present context, moreover, the rule does not have the special status of a law; it is not cited by Ajax as having any special authority, and Achilles is not persuaded to follow it. Of course the rule might be cited (along with others) in a court case, such as the one portrayed on Achilles' shield, where two men are disputing about blood-money for a man who has been killed,[33] but the tag "as Ajax says" or "as Homer says" would not give the rule any compelling authority in such a case. To the extent that Ajax's generalization accurately represents the behavior of most members of the society and to the extent that Homer (or Ajax) was highly regarded, citation of the rule may have some persuasive force in a legal or other context. But a law is something different from a sociological observation.[34] This rule cannot be considered a law simply because it might be true,[35] unless it is explicitly differentiated from other rules in Homer that are not laws, and clearly no such differentiation exists.[36] In short,

33. *Iliad* 18.497–508; we shall examine this famous scene in the next chapter.
34. See Hart 1961, 86–88 on the internal and external aspects of rules.
35. In fact in Homer the acceptance of blood-money after a homicide is extremely rare. A more accurate statement of the situation is Odysseus's remark to Telemachus after the slaughter of the suitors: "Someone who has killed only one man in a community, for whom only a few avengers are left, nonetheless flees, leaving his kinsmen and country" (*Od.* 23.118–20). See the catalogue of epic homicides in Gagarin 1981a, 6–10. Like Odysseus, Phoenix also uses a false generalization in his speech to Achilles. He says that when a man does wrong, he may appease the anger of the gods with sacrifices (*Il.* 9.497–501). The epics provide ample evidence to the contrary.
36. Compare, for example, the general observation made by the disguised Athena to Odysseus in *Od.* 7.51–52: "The bold man comes out better in everything, even if he comes from a foreign land." This is also a generalization intended to persuade, but we would certainly not call it a law. In fact, there are relatively few explicitly

laws must have a special position among the rules of a society, and this is normally possible only when they are written.

This analysis of the development of law in three main stages has been motivated partly by the conviction that legal procedures in a preliterate society may be defined more easily than legal rules. The analysis further implies that formal procedures for settling disputes may come into existence and be recognized before any of the society's rules are formally recognized as legal rules. This is not always the case, but it is a possible pattern and one that we shall find when we examine the emergence of law in early Greece.

This conclusion in turn suggests that we may wish to revise the traditional understanding of substantive law as somehow "primary" law and procedural law as "secondary" or "adjective" law, to use Bentham's term.[37] Bentham and most later scholars[38] think of law primarily in terms of a rule-violation model, according to which substantive rules could theoretically exist by themselves without any procedures to redress violations, but procedural rules could not exist alone since their function is to help provide redress in case of violations of substantive rules. But even on this model, procedures for redressing violations may be formally recognized and even stated in writing before the rules subject to these procedures are formally recognized. And if we think more generally in terms of dispute settlement, it is easy to see how procedures for settling disputes might

---

stated rules of behavior in Homer; most social rules are only implicit in people's speeches or must be inferred from examples (see Havelock 1978, esp. 106–22).

37. See Bentham (written ca. 1780): "There are then two sorts of laws: one of which are altogether principal without being subsidiary to any: the other subsidiary and principal at the same time. As to these latter however the subsidiary character is that in which they . . . not only could not have any effect, but they could not be understood, nor even have existence, without having a principal law to refer to: the idea of such a law being included in their very essence . . . Those laws then which cannot stand alone, but require to be preceded by some other to which they may adhere, may on that account be styled *adjective* or *enclitic* laws: those of the opposite description, *substantive* or *self-subsisting*. To the adjective class belong all laws relative to the course of judiciary procedure" (Hart 1970, 141–42).

38. See, for example, the discussion in Salmond 1913, 437–40, which, like most such discussions, treats substantive law as an end and procedural law as simply a means to that end (see pp. 72–73 below). Procedure has, as one might expect, been granted a higher status by the realists; see, e.g., Llewellyn 1951, 17–18, who plays down the separation of substantive from procedural law and emphasizes the latter *"as conditioning the existence of any substantive law at all"* (his emphasis); see also Calhoun 1944, 13–14.

arise without any reference to or dependence on substantive rules, whether written or not. Thus it may be more accurate to view procedural law as primary and substantive law as a later development.[39]

That procedural law need not be subsidiary to substantive law is easily proven by a number of actual cases. For example, the first written collection of Roman laws, the Twelve Tables (ca. 450 B.C.), begins with a fundamental law of procedure: "If a man summons another to court, he shall go; if he does not go, the plaintiff shall first summon a witness and then take the defendant by force." Coming as it does at the head of a code, this procedural law must be independent of any substantive law. Other examples of collections of written laws beginning with a procedural regulation are the Great Code at Gortyn and the laws of Hammurabi.[40] That these ancient codes begin with important procedural laws suggests that procedure may have a higher status, at least in early laws, than is generally recognized.[41]

39. I do not mean to imply that procedural law is primary in a metaphysical sense (though I think this could be argued); I only mean that it may be formally expressed or recognized earlier than substantive law. Procedural laws standing alone, such as those discussed below, may contain an implicit reference to unexpressed substantive rights, and in many cases the procedural and substantive guarantees of a right cannot be completely separated. For our purposes, however, it is significant that in some cases, at least, procedural laws may be formalized independently of and earlier than substantive law.

40. The opening of the Gortyn Code is discussed on page 96. The first five sections of Hammurabi's laws deal with what Driver and Miles (1952, 43) call "offenses against the administration of justice" (false charges, false testimony, and falsification of judgment). Note that the remaining 277 sections of Hammurabi's code contain only substantive laws. Other early codes that begin with procedural regulations are the Laws of Manu and the Lex Salica. These codes have all been conveniently collected in Kocourek and Wigmore 1915.

41. Cf. Bohannan's analysis (1965, esp. 45–50), according to which in every society there exist legal institutions for settling disputes that arise within the context of the other institutions in the society. These legal institutions have rules governing their own activities (i.e., procedural rules) and also rules "that are substitutions or modifications or restatements of the rules" of nonlegal institutions (i.e., substantive rules). For the rules of other institutions to become laws they must be made rules of the legal institution as well. Before becoming "doubly institutionalized," they are simply customs. Marriage customs, for example, become marriage laws when they are formally stated or recognized as rules by the society's legal institutions. In our schema societies at the proto-legal stage of development have legal institutions governed by certain rules and thus have procedural law, but they have not yet doubly institutionalized the customs of other institutions and thus do not yet have substantive law.

The analysis of law in terms of the primacy of legal procedure has some interesting implications. Since a legal procedure requires at least two legally recognized parties, rules governing the behavior of one person alone cannot be legal rules, at least not until the state presents itself as a legal party whose interests may be harmed by, say, the smoking of marijuana. The presence of two parties in a legal procedure may be a significant factor in the separation of laws from other rules of behavior in a society. Consider the treatment of homicide in the Homeric poems,[42] where the normal result of a homicide is that the killer goes into exile, often because he is pursued or threatened with pursuit by the victim's relatives. There are two clear exceptions to this rule. First, Heracles kills his houseguest, Iphitus, desiring to obtain his horses (*Odyssey* 21.24–30), but since Iphitus is a foreigner and has no family present to seek revenge on his behalf, Heracles suffers no material penalty, though he does incur the anger of Zeus. Apparently the killing of a foreigner who was a guest in one's house resulted at this period in no legal dispute and thus no legal punishment. It was considered a religious or moral violation —an offense against the laws of hospitality guaranteed by Zeus— but not a legal (or proto-legal) violation.[43] Second, Oedipus in the version of the story known to Homer (*Odyssey* 11.271–80; cf. *Iliad* 23.679–80) continued to rule in Thebes after it became known that he killed his father, and he apparently suffered no punishment for this deed. Here too there was no living relative who could seek vengeance on behalf of the victim.

It would be misleading to say that the Greeks had a law against killing members of one's own community but no law against killing

---

Bohannan's discussion also provides a means for differentiating between substantive and procedural law, since we may often distinguish fairly clearly between the rules of a society's legal institutions and those other rules which have been doubly institutionalized.

42. The evidence for the treatment of homicide in the epics is examined in Gagarin 1981a, 6–18.

43. Much the same can be said of killing a beggar or a suppliant, who would also have no family present to seek revenge on their behalf. Cf. the story related in the (seventh-century?) *Aethiopis* (see Proclus, *Chrest.* 2) that Achilles killed Thersites and was later purified by Odysseus on the island of Lesbos. From Proclus's brief summary it is impossible to determine the reasons for this. Apparently Thersites had no family or supporters powerful enough to demand a more severe punishment. See Parker 1983, 130–31.

foreigners or one's own closest relatives, though an attempt to deduce "laws" from the material of the epic poems might lead one to this conclusion. We can, however, say that the general prohibition against killing within the community arose in the first place (and later became a law) because the killing of another member of one's community gave rise to a dispute which had to be settled and which thus required a legal procedure. Only later did the Greeks develop forms of legal procedure to cover other cases of homicide, such as the killing of a foreigner, and even in fourth-century Athens one could sometimes avoid a prosecution for homicide if the victim died without any surviving relative or other person with the status to prosecute.[44] In sum, those anthropologists who speak about laws as those rules subject to adjudication by a court have a valid point if we treat this criterion as a necessary but not a sufficient condition;[45] we still need a rule of recognition in order to determine which of these rules are (strictly speaking) laws.

These Homeric examples suggest a rather clear separation between law and religion in their early stages. A common view of law, which has persisted since the earliest comparative legal studies, is that the earliest law (or "pre-law") is strongly religious, only becoming fully secular in its later historical development.[46] Whatever validity this view might have with respect to other societies, we shall

44. The *locus classicus* is Demosthenes 47.68–73, for a full discussion of which see Gagarin 1979.

45. See, for instance, the examples Schapera (1938, 37–38) cites in distinguishing legal rules as those which are, or could be, adjudicated in court: on the one hand the rule against intercourse with another man's wife, violations of which are a matter for a court to settle, and on the other hand the "taboo" against intercourse with one's own wife during menstruation, violations of which require ritual purification but would not result in any legal action. In the first case a violation results in a conflict between two legally recognized parties, the violator and the woman's husband; in the second case there is no such conflict, since the woman has no legal standing, and the offense thus gives rise to no dispute which can be legally settled. Schapera classifies this latter rule as a religious taboo.

46. In the famous words of Maine: "the severance of law from morality, and of religion from law, belongs very distinctly to the later stages of mental progress" (1861, 9). Unlike some of his successors, however, Maine does not emphasize the religious nature of early law so much as the undifferentiated nature of law and religion at the earliest stages. For the religious nature of early Greek law, see Latte 1920 and the classic study by Gernet, "Droit et prédroit en grèce ancienne" in Gernet 1968, 175–260. The theory attributed to Maine of a close connection between early law and religion is strongly opposed by Diamond 1971.

see that religious factors are of little significance in the earliest stages of Greek law.

My intent in these preliminary remarks has been primarily to explore some possible senses in which we may speak of law in preliterate society and to provide a framework, or model, for an examination of the emergence of law in preclassical Greece. The conclusions reached will, I hope, be helpful for this particular purpose. I do not claim that they will necessarily help in understanding other societies or that they provide an adequate analysis of the development of law in general. I do believe, however, that the study of Greek law, especially at its earliest stages, can shed light on some of the more general issues discussed above. Although it should be studied first as an important aspect of Greek culture, the study of Greek law can and should both draw upon and contribute to the more general study of law in human society, and I have tried to make the following study comprehensible and of interest to both classicists and nonclassicists. Unfortunately, although there are signs the situation may be changing,[47] those who have studied Greek law have rarely been concerned to communicate their work to other legal historians, legal theorists, or anthropologists.[48]

The Greeks present us with a special situation. Although our evidence may be quite limited, it is "indigenous" in that not only at the earliest stages, but even up through the classical period Greek law developed, as far as we can tell, without any significant external influences.[49] The Greek evidence extends, moreover, over a considerable period of time, from the proto-legal stage through several centuries of law in the full sense. Few other societies provide us with evidence for such a full range of the development of a legal system. For Rome we have virtually no evidence for the period before the

47. See the recent work of Humphreys (1983, 1985a, 1985b) and Cantarella's 1979 study of "norms and sanctions" in Homer.

48. The most notable exceptions to these general comments on the study of Greek law are the works of Louis Gernet (see especially Gernet 1955, 1968), who was thoroughly trained in anthropology as well as the Classics (see Humphreys 1978, 76–106), and of H. J. Wolff, who in addition to writing dozens of specialized studies has continually sought to communicate his interest in Greek law to nonspecialists (see, for instance, Wolff 1975); for an excellent appraisal of Wolff's work, see Thür 1984. The best recent work on Greek law is MacDowell's survey of Athenian law (MacDowell 1978), which is accessible to nonclassicists.

49. See Headlam 1892–93, 48–49. On the possibility of Near Eastern influence on early Greek laws see below, especially pp. 126–29.

first written laws. In England and on the Continent many early codes of law survive, but almost all of these already show the influence from Roman or canon law (though the common law may have been relatively untouched by this influence).[50] In African and other primitive societies the legal systems studied by anthropologists have usually come under the influence of Western law.

On the other hand, the evidence for Greek law, especially for the archaic period, is quantitatively slight and often of doubtful worth. Indeed, some may feel that even the best-documented period of Athenian law—the fifth and fourth centuries—does not offer sufficient evidence, and that for the archaic period any attempt to draw conclusions about the development of law is futile. Although I obviously do not subscribe to such scepticism, we must always bear in mind that the views set forth in the following chapters must remain tentative. The effort to understand the emergence of law in archaic Greece is worthwhile nonetheless, and even a partial understanding of its function in that society can shed light on the culture as a whole.

50. For England see Pollock and Maitland 1898, 1: cii. Richardson and Sayles argue (1966, 1–4), however, that the first article of the oldest laws, those of Aethelbehrt (ca. A.D. 600), is an interpolation, and that none of the remaining articles shows any influence from the church. Note that Aethelbehrt's laws are entirely substantive (torts and marriage law); there is not a word about procedure, which presumably was controlled by the king and his officers. On the early Germanic codes see Watson 1985, 77–89.

2

THE SETTLEMENT OF DISPUTES
IN EARLY GREEK
LITERATURE

I have suggested in the preceding chapter that in the development of a society formal procedures for settling disputes peacefully may arise before any rules are written down as statutory laws. This was certainly the order of events in Greece. The Greeks learned—or more precisely relearned—the art of writing in about the middle of the eighth century B.C., and all the evidence, which we shall examine in Chapters 3 and 4, indicates that they began writing laws about the middle of the seventh century.[1] By this time their earliest literary works, the poems of Homer and Hesiod, had already achieved their final form,[2] and these poems, as we shall see, contain clear evidence for the existence of formal, public means of settling disputes. The evidence of Athenian history, moreover, confirms this pattern of development, since we hear of trials and the recording of decisions by the *thesmothetai* in the period before Draco gave the Athenians their first written laws.[3] It thus appears certain that rec-

1. For the date of the introduction of writing to Greece, see Jeffery 1961a, 12–21 (and now Jeffery 1982); see also Coldstream 1977, 295–302 and Snodgrass 1980, 78–84.

2. For the dates of the poems of Homer and Hesiod, see West 1966, 40–48; his view that the *Theogony* is earlier than the Homeric poems has not found many supporters, but there is general agreement that all these poems were given their final form by about 700 B.C. or not much later. Janko (1982, 228–31) is inclined to place Hesiod's works in the first half of the seventh century. A sixth century date for the final composition of the Homeric poems has recently been argued by Jensen 1980, but this view has won little support.

3. The Cylonian conspiracy, during which a trial was apparently proposed for the conspirators, is commonly dated to 636 or 632, at least a decade before Draco wrote his laws (but see Levy 1978). Aristotle mentions trials by the early archons (*Ath. Pol.* 3.5) as well as the recording of decisions by the *thesmothetai* (*Ath. Pol.* 3.4); for the latter see Gagarin 1981b and chap. 3 below.

ognized legal procedures had already developed in Greece before legal rules were written down and officially recognized. The evidence for this conclusion is entirely literary. Of course literary evidence is not straightforward sociological or anthropological documentation, and some have questioned the use of Homeric and other poetry to shed light on the social institutions of early Greece. But most scholars now feel that these poems do reflect fairly accurately Greek society during the century or so preceding their final composition and may thus be used with care as evidence for social conditions at the end of the Dark Ages.[4] I shall also make use of some literary evidence from the later, literate period, since this helps to clarify and support the picture drawn from the earlier evidence. Despite some variation in detail, the different examples of this procedure show enough similarity to indicate the existence of a well-established, traditional procedure. Thus all the evidence down to the first half of the fifth century demonstrates that before the introduction of writing the Greeks had established a formal, public procedure for settling disputes.

The basic elements in this procedure can most easily be grasped if we begin not with the earliest literature but with a story in Herodotus (1.96–98) about Deioces, the first king of the Medes. Although Herodotus is not relating Greek history, the story seems, nonetheless, to be shaped by Greek thinking about law and order and to be relevant to the Greek experience.[5] Herodotus relates that Deioces, a wise man, wanted to become tyrant of the Medes, who at that time lived "autonomously" in scattered villages. Accordingly, though he already had a high reputation in his own village, he prac-

4. See Finley 1978, esp. 142–58, and Havelock 1978, 55–87. As Diamant (1982, 44) puts it after reviewing all the evidence, "the world of Odysseus is the world of Geometric Greece" (i.e., the ninth and eighth centuries B.C.). This is not to say that Homer is portraying a real society in every detail, but rather that despite possible inconsistencies or anomalies (see, e.g., Snodgrass 1974; Geddes 1984) his picture of social institutions reflects those of this period. My argument, in any case, does not depend on the identification of "Homeric society" with any single period, but only on the assumption that the judicial process portrayed in the epics (and in other works) was established in Greece by the time these poems achieved their final form.

5. I do not mean to deny the historical existence of Deioces, but the details of Herodotus's version of his rise to power probably reflect fifth-century Greek views of the origins of social order, just as the details he includes in the famous debate among the Persians about constitutions (3.80–82) certainly reflect Greek political thinking of the fifth century. Protagoras's myth of the origin of social order (Plato, *Prot.* 320C–322A) shows some interesting similarities to the story of Deioces.

ticed *dikaiosynē* ("justice")[6] even more zealously. There was considerable lawlessness (*anomiē*) throughout the country at the time and when the people of Deioces' own village observed his qualities, "they chose him (repeatedly) to be their judge."[7] Since he was "straight" (*ithys*) and "just" (*dikaios*), he rapidly gained a reputation as the only one who judged cases "correctly" (*kata to orthon*). Soon people in other villages, who had previously encountered unjust decisions from judges in their own villages, began to come to Deioces to have their cases judged, and in the end they would take their disputes to no one else. More and more people came to him, but one day Deioces refused to sit where he had formerly sat giving judgments and said he would no longer decide cases. It did him no good, he said, to neglect his own affairs and spend all day deciding cases for his neighbors. Pillaging and lawlessness now flourished more than ever, so that finally the Medes had no choice but to hold a council and appoint Deioces king.

From this brief story the following picture of the settlement of disputes in an early (proto-legal) society emerges: at a particular place in each village one or more men would regularly sit and decide cases, though these "judges" attended to other matters as well. These cases would be brought to them by litigants, who could select any judge they wished and could even go to another village to get their disputes settled. If they could not find an acceptable judge, many disputes would go unsettled and lawlessness[8] would increase. Those judges with a reputation for "straight" decisions would have many cases to decide; those with the opposite reputation would have few.

We may infer from these details that the decision to submit a dispute to a particular judge must have been a voluntary one, supported by both parties. If one litigant alone could compel a case to

6. For *dikaiosynē* here and elsewhere in fifth-century literature, see Havelock 1969.

7. δικαστὴν ἑωυτῶν αἱρέοντο. This phrase is commonly translated to imply that people chose Deioces once and for all to be their judge, but the imperfect tense indicates that they must have kept on choosing him each time they needed a dispute settled.

8. "Lawlessness" (*anomiē*) does not here denote either the absence of laws (*nomoi*) or the violation of specific laws, but rather indicates behavior that is violent and opposed to *nomos* in the sense of "law and order" (see Ostwald 1969, 85–95). When disputes cannot be settled peacefully, then conflicts will necessarily become violent and the established social order will disintegrate.

be heard by a particular judge, then "unjust" judges would not be short of cases to hear, since a litigant with a weak case who had his choice in the matter would presumably not take his case to a judge with a high reputation for straight decisions, but rather to one who was known to be biased or corrupt or simply stupid. Only when both litigants participated in the selection would they consistently seek out the best judge, as happened in Deioces' case.

A consequence of such a system is that a judge's reputation for "straight judgments" must have depended on his ability to render decisions acceptable to both sides. At least he must have done so most of the time, or else both parties in other similar disputes would not appeal to him. We may further infer that litigants generally wanted "just" settlements for their disputes. In most disputes, therefore, each party must have felt his own case had some validity. For example, a man might seize another man's cow as payment for a debt or in settlement of some grievance, and the ensuing dispute could be submitted to a judge for settlement with each litigant feeling he had a valid case. A man who stole a cow with no justification, however, was probably someone who did not accept the social order and would not agree to submit his case to any judge with a reputation for fairness. If caught, he would probably be dealt with outside the judicial system.[9]

A judge who satisfied both litigants most of the time would gain a reputation for "justice," and once such a judge became well known, all those who basically accepted the social order and wished to have their disputes with their neighbors settled peacefully would naturally resort to this judge. After a while, moreover, the force of public opinion would probably exert pressure even on those with relatively weak cases to submit their disputes to this judge or else be publicly discredited. Thus a basically voluntary procedure could be additionally supported by the force of public opinion, given a judge whose general fairness was recognized. Without such a judge the whole system would break down.[10]

9. One may speculate that such criminals were termed κακοῦργοι ("malefactors") and that, since an ordinary *dikē* would not be effective in these cases, a different procedure, the *apagōgē* or "summary arrest," was developed in Athens in order to bring them to justice. The procedure is probably at least as old as Draco; see p. 113, n. 35, below.

10. Cf. Hesiod's view (*WD* 238–47) that a corrupt or malfunctioning legal process will lead to the ruin of the whole society.

Although such a system may seem strange to us,[11] it has parallels in tribal societies.[12] Its purpose is not so much to punish violations of rules as to settle disputes and thus eliminate or at least lessen strife in a society. In such a system the main requirement for a judge is not that he know the law, in the sense of knowing the precise rules of behavior in the society. To be sure, he, like every other member of the society, will know these rules; but more importantly he must show the wisdom to find a settlement based on these rules that both parties will see as fair, or at least be persuaded to accept. Such wisdom is especially necessary in the settlement of disputes not involving the simple violation of a rule but rather the conflict of two or more rules. In such conflicts each party may feel, perhaps with justification, that his case is valid, and the settlement will thus normally be in the nature of a compromise rather than a complete victory for one side. The task of the judge is to find a "straight" settlement—one, that is, that fairly divides the legitimate claims of both sides.[13] Few people will have this judicial skill, and thus the talents of a man like Deioces were highly valued.

It is clear that Deioces was no "lawgiver." There is no mention of his instituting new *nomoi* (whether written laws or unwritten cus-

11. Note, however, that Plato (*Laws* 767B) establishes a court where both sides choose the judges themselves (i.e., an arbitration court) as κυριώτατος, which may perhaps be translated "most authoritative" (but see England 1921, ad loc.).

12. "Some of them [the people who became subjects of the Alur] even asked an Alur chief to give them one of his sons as their ruler; and one of their principal reasons for wanting a ruler was so that he could settle their quarrels" (Mair 1962, 52). "Both [parties] should . . . concur in the decision, and each must agree . . . to carry out his part of it. If such concurrence and agreement are not obtained, the case will probably be said to have been settled arbitrarily. . . . No chief . . . who develops a reputation for such arbitrary rulings can long retain his prestige or his influence" (Bohannan 1957, 19; see also n. 36 below). "Many writers have discussed the process of law in tribal societies in such phrases as restoring the social balance or equilibrium, securing the agreement of both parties to a compromise judgment and, above all, reconciling the parties. This is the main aim of Barotse judges in all cases that arise between kin, for it is a dominant value of the society that villages should not break up and that kin should remain united" (Gluckman 1965a, 9). Cf. Köhler on the Hebrew institution of "justice in the gate" (i.e., judgments rendered at the city's gate): "This activity of judgment is understood to be that of giving assistance to justice. To judge does not mean establishing the facts of a criminal offence and then judging and sentencing on the basis of this establishment of fact, but, in Hebrew, 'to judge' and 'to help' are parallel ideas" (1956, 156).

13. A "straight" *dikē* may originally have been a boundary mark evenly dividing two pieces of property; see Palmer 1950.

toms), or changing old *nomoi;* these presumably remained as they were. His contribution was purely procedural. The story implies, moreover, that a properly functioning legal procedure was vitally important for the well-being of the society, more important even than a good set of rules of behavior. Finally, it is interesting to note that after Deioces is firmly established in power, he begins to "judge" his subjects' behavior somewhat differently:[14] he secludes himself in his palace and hands down written decisions on cases presented to him in writing. He also sends informants throughout the land so that people can be properly punished for their wrongs (*adikēmata*). Herodotus seems to suggest that the establishment of a single authoritative ruler alters the nature of a country's judicial system.

Taken by itself this story has no necessary relevance to the question of legal procedure in early Greece, but when we examine the earlier literature, particularly Homer and Hesiod, we find that the picture it presents of legal procedure in early Greece corresponds closely to Herodotus's picture of Deioces. Consider first a passage in the proem of Hesiod's *Theogony,* where he extols the benefits the Muses confer on kings (80–93). If the Muses favor a king, Hesiod says, "soothing words flow from his mouth" (84). It has seemed odd to some that a king should be said to have the gift of the Muses,[15] but the subsequent lines make Hesiod's sense quite clear: "And all the people look at him, deciding the proprieties with straight settlements.[16] And he, speaking surely, quickly and intelligently puts an end to even a great dispute. Therefore there are intelligent kings,[17] in order that in the agora [the public meeting or market place] they may easily restore matters for people who have suffered damages, persuading them with gentle words" (84–90).

From these lines several points emerge. The gift of the Muses benefits a king specifically in deciding cases; the king's settlement

14. Herodotus 1.100.

15. Several different explanations of this alleged oddity are mentioned by Verdenius (1972, 251–2).

16. διακρίνοντα θέμιστας / ἰθείῃσι δίκῃσιν (*Th.* 85–86). I take the *themistes* to be norms of behavior. They are elsewhere said, together with the *skēptron* to be the gift of Zeus (e.g., *Il.* 2.205–6), but this does not mean that the king's task in Hesiod's view is simply to determine the will of Zeus, as Wolff says (1980, 570). Wolff links the ascription of *themistes* to Zeus with the ascription of early Codes to a god (see chap. 3 below). The purpose of these ascriptions, I would argue, is to strengthen the people's perception of the validity of the king's settlement or the new Codes. On "straight" settlements see West 1966, ad loc. (see n. 13 above, and n. 83 below).

17. For this interpretation of a difficult construction, see West 1966, ad loc.

was pronounced orally; the settlement should be an intelligent one that restores matters to their original condition if someone has suffered damages; and finally, the king persuades the litigants to accept the settlement. This last function requires the help of the Muses.

The Muses' great gift to a king is thus the ability to speak well in pronouncing his decisions and in persuading litigants to accept it and cease their strife. Of course the decision must basically be an intelligent one, which provides adequate restitution for loss. But it must also be accepted by the litigants. Hesiod's kings appear to be working within the same sort of system as Herodotus portrays, namely one in which litigants voluntarily (though perhaps under the pressure of public opinion) bring their disputes to judges[18] to be settled and where at least for the most part settlements must be acceptable to both parties. Thus the need for persuasive speech: the king does not simply deliver an authoritative judgment; he must persuade the parties to a dispute that his settlement is truly a straight one.[19]

In a recent study of this passage, Roth agrees that this is Hesiod's understanding of the Muses' gift, but argues that he has misunderstood the relationship between the kings and the Muses.[20] Her hypothesis (and she does not claim that it is anything more than that) is that the kings memorized an oral collection of legal rules (*dikai*), which they passed on to their successors. In support of this theory she cites alleged parallels from other early Indo-European societies, particularly early Ireland,[21] but presents little direct evidence from Greece.

In assessing this hypothesis one must first consider the absence of

18. Although Hesiod does not explicitly indicate that several "kings" are available for the litigants to approach, this seems to be the implication of his frequent use of the plural both here and in *WD* 213–85 (see below). Clearly these "kings" were relatively minor nobles; see West 1978 on *WD* 38 and n. 69 below.

19. The passage is correctly understood by Solmsen: "The kings whom Hesiod here has in mind do not *impose* judgments but rely on their gift of gentle persuasion . . . to settle their disputes" (1954, 7).

20. Roth 1976, 338.

21. Roth relies heavily on Benveniste's discussion of the etymology of *dikē* (Benveniste 1973, 385–88). Benveniste's whole discussion seems to be predicated on a false idea of "what we know of codes of law among peoples of a traditional civilization, collections of oral pronouncements, which are centred round the relations of kinship, of the clan and the tribe" (387). As we noted in chap. 1, however, the existence of any oral codes of law is questionable; at most they are found in only one or two early societies. And there is no evidence for a concept of "unwritten laws" in Greece earlier than the fifth century; see p. 55, n. 13, below.

Greek evidence for orally preserved collections of laws. Although Roth is correct in identifying the style of early written Greek laws as conditional sentences written in condensed prose,[22] this style is in fact quite different from that of either the Hesiodic maxims she cites[23] or the Spartan *rhētra*, which seems to preserve traces of orality. And the report that the Spartan king Lycurgus required all citizens to memorize the laws is beside the point, since Sparta was clearly exceptional among Greek cities in prohibiting written laws.[24] The strongest argument against Roth's hypothesis, however, is the *Theogony* passage she is interpreting (*Th.* 77–103). It is simply incredible that Hesiod, with his evident first-hand knowledge of the kings and their procedures for judging cases, could have so misunderstood the nature of their work. If Hesiod says that the Muses give kings the gift of persuasive eloquence in order to persuade litigants to settle their disputes, he must know that this is their special function. He makes no mention of any memorization or recital of a body of rules, and without any other evidence for such activity in ancient Greece, we must clearly reject the theory that Hesiod's kings memorized oral laws. Hesiod's words, like the other passages we must now consider, thus confirm the picture of early Greek legal procedure presented in Herodotus's story of Deioces.[25]

The clearest and strongest evidence for the existence of a formal, public legal procedure in preliterate Greece is the trial scene on Achilles' shield (*Iliad* 18.497–508):[26]

> A crowd, then, in a market place, and there
> two men at odds over satisfaction owed
> for a murder done: one claimed that all was paid,

22. See further Gagarin 1981a, 153–61.

23. Roth (1976, 335–36) cites *WD* 707–13, a second-person address with none of the ellipsis common in early laws.

24. On the *rhētra* and the prohibition of written laws in Sparta, see chap. 3 below.

25. I am not asserting that memory was of no importance at all for Hesiod's kings; it may have been very helpful to them to remember previous cases and settlements. Among the Tiruray the official negotiators of settlements (called *kefeduwan*) are often known for their ability to remember small details of cases settled decades earlier (Schlegel 1970, 59–60). Cf. p. 131 below on the "rememberers" in Greece.

26. Among the many treatments of this scene see Bonner and Smith 1930, 31–41, Wolff 1946, 34–49, Hommel 1969, Thür 1970, MacDowell 1978, 18–21, and Ruschenbusch 1982, all with further bibliography.

and publicly declared it; his opponent
turned the reparation down, and both
demanded a verdict from an arbiter,
as people clamored in support of each,
and criers restrained the crowd. The town elders
sat in a ring, on chairs of polished stone,
the staves [skēptra] of clarion criers in their hands,
with which they sprang up, each to speak in turn,
and in the middle were two golden measures
to be awarded to him whose argument
would be the most straightforward.

(trans. Fitzgerald)[27]

Although there is much disagreement on the details of this brief scene, it is reasonably certain that the two litigants have voluntarily submitted their dispute for settlement and that they plead their case in a public forum (in the agora) to a circle of elders, each of whom in turn takes a scepter (a symbol of public authority),[28] stands, and pronounces a settlement. Clearly this is a formal, public procedure, providing a means for litigants to bring their disputes to an authoritative body for settlement.

H. J. Wolff, in an important and influential examination of this scene, has disputed the natural implication of verse 501 ("both demanded a verdict") that the submission of the dispute is fully voluntary.[29] He argues that the "defendant" (i.e., the killer) has sought protection against the forceful use of self-help (i.e., against being

27. I use Fitzgerald's translation of this passage (1974, 451) because he, unlike Lattimore, preserves many of the ambiguities of the Greek text.

28. Cf. Havelock (with reference to the dispute between Agamemnon and Achilles): "The performance of judgment is also a function of rhetoric: the one is achieved through the other, so that the scepter is both a judge's symbol and a speaker's symbol" (1978, 133). Gernet calls the scepter "un symbole de puissance religieuse" (1968, 240), but although it was originally given as a gift from Zeus (see *Il.* 2.101–8) and its use suggests a royal authority often said to be derived from Zeus, in no passage in Homer is the scepter used in a clearly religious context. Mondi (1980) also argues for the existence of divine kingship, symbolized by the *skēptron*, in early Greece but admits that the Homeric poems preserve only "a dimming memory" (211) of this alleged identification of king and god. Cf. Calhoun: "The king enjoys the special favour and protection of Zeus; this is undoubtedly a heritage from the patriarchate and in no way implies a doctrine of divine right" (1962, 436).

29. ἄμφω δ᾽ ἱέσθην . . . πεῖραρ ἑλέσθαι (18.501); see Wolff 1946, 34–49.

killed in retaliation) by the "plaintiff," that a powerful member of
the society has provided this protection, which is sanctioned by the
community, and that protection will continue to be provided until
the plaintiff wins a court judgment allowing him to continue his use
of self-help. Thus (in Wolff's view) the plaintiff is not, strictly speaking, forced to present his case in court, but until he does, the community will protect the defendant, and he therefore agrees to present
his case in court.

This theory has won considerable support among scholars,[30] but
the strongest evidence Wolff adduces in its support, namely that the
"defendant" apparently speaks first, is hardly enough to overturn
the clear implication of verse 501, particularly in view of the abundant evidence for voluntary procedure in Homer, Hesiod, and other
early literature. Moreover, there is no evidence that the community
or one of its representatives might protect a killer if the victim's relatives do not agree to submit the dispute for judgment. It is by no
means certain that Homer intends to portray the "defendant" as
speaking first, and even the terms "plaintiff" and "defendant" are
misleading and probably inappropriate for describing the litigants
not only in this scene but also in the other disputes we shall consider below in which both parties appear to have grievances (Hesiod
and Perses, Hermes and Apollo).[31] This is not a homicide case in
which a victim is suing an offender for damages, but rather a dispute over "satisfaction owed" (poinē), in which both parties appear
to have some grievance. Thus we have every reason to accept the
implication of verse 501 that both litigants voluntarily present their
dispute for settlement.

An interesting variation of Wolff's interpretation of this scene has
recently been proposed by Thür, who argues that each elder pro-

30. E.g., Harrison 1972, 69–72; Ruschenbusch (1982) following Wolff, suggests
analogies with later Athenian procedure, in particular the treatment of adultery,
where an adulterer who is wrongly entrapped by self-help can prosecute his en-
trapper. Nothing in Homer's text, however, suggests a dispute over the propriety of
using self-help, nor is there any indication that the "plaintiff" (the original killer, in
Wolff's view) disputes either that the crime took place or that he is guilty of it.

31. Although Hesiod sees himself as the injured party, it makes little sense to
speak of him as the "plaintiff." In the *Hymn to Hermes* (see below), although the
primary offender is clearly Hermes, he is the one who first suggests taking the case to
Zeus for settlement, but Apollo speaks his case first. Similarly, as Thür observes
(1970, 430), Menelaus speaks first in his dispute with Antilochus, but in that case
too the terms "plaintiff" and "defendant" are best avoided.

poses not a settlement of the dispute but rather a method of proof (*Beweisverfahren*), by means of which the dispute will automatically be settled.[32] These methods of proof, which are essentially irrational and were thought to depend on the intervention of the gods, include the oath, the ordeal, and combat, all known from early Germanic law. According to Thür, the dispute concerns a simple matter of fact, whether or not the *poinē* has been paid, and the outcome cannot be a compromise, which would be unfair to the litigant who is telling the truth, but must result in the victory of one party by means of an automatic proof. Thür accepts Wolff's view that this judicial proceeding intervenes in the system of self-help by either allowing or denying the injured party his right of revenge. But he maintains that this right and the defendant's safety before the trial are guaranteed by the society as a whole rather than by an individual protector.

The main objections to this theory are that there is no hint of such a procedure in the description of this scene,[33] and that even on the doubtful assumption that the dispute concerns only a simple matter of fact (see below), there would seem to be no reason for the existence of such a complex procedure merely in order to decide upon a method of proof. There is no good evidence that the Greeks ever used the methods of ordeal and combat,[34] and even if they did, it is hard to imagine a group of distinguished elders competing to see which could propose the most acceptable of three possible methods of proof, or that a prize of two talents would be awarded to the winner. It is also hard to imagine that two litigants (and their

32. Thür 1970; a similar view is advanced by Primmer 1970, though he focuses on the dispute between Menelaus and Antilochus (see below) and deals only briefly with the scene on Achilles' shield.

33. See Talamanca 1979, 111–13 and passim. Thür claims to find evidence for such a procedure in the dispute between Menelaus and Antilochus, on which see below.

34. I can find no evidence for combat in a legal situation in Greece. The duel between Paris and Menelaus in the *Iliad* is clearly meant to decide the war and is presented as such, despite the fact that there is a potential legal dispute between the two. All the other examples of "trial by combat" discussed by Armstrong (1950) similarly involve military rather than legal situations. Thus they are not evidence for trial by combat as a legal procedure. Latte (1920, 6–7) argues that the watchman's words in *Antigone* 264–67 ("I would hold red-hot metal in my hands, or walk through fire, or swear an oath to the gods . . .") are a reflection of an early use of ordeal in Greek legal procedure but they may better be taken as a reflection of methods of extracting or confirming information from slaves.

supporters) who disagreed about a straightforward factual matter would be able to agree on a method of proof, since any method would likely favor one party or the other. It is unlikely, moreover, that the polis at this time was a powerful enough entity to protect a defendant against a plaintiff who demanded his revenge, or that the polis could insist that the defendant obtain a legal verdict in his favor in order to claim this protection.

Finally, though the gods play a significant role in the Homeric epics, the idea of leaving a decision in a dispute between mortals entirely in the hands of an irrational, automatic, divinely determined procedure is completely absent from the poems and seems to violate the basically humanistic spirit of all Greek thought from Homer on. The many other passages we shall consider below all indicate that men could submit their disputes for a settlement that would be delivered by a judge and agreed to by the litigants. To the extent that Homer provides details, precisely such a procedure seems to be envisioned in the scene on Achilles' shield. The only significant variation from the procedure already described is that the individual judges are grouped into a body of judges, from among whose opinions one will be selected as the final settlement. However, this body functions as a group of individuals, and the final settlement is apparently that of one judge only.

Just how this settlement is achieved is not certain, but it is generally accepted that the two measures of gold are a prize for the elder who speaks the straightest settlement (*dikē*).[35] Assuming this is correct, what is meant by the "straightest *dikē*" and how is it determined? In the system of voluntary submission of disputes for settlement outlined above, it seems likely that the straightest *dikē* is the settlement most acceptable to the two litigants, though they are undoubtedly influenced by the approval of the attending crowd and the opinions of the other elders. Many examples from African societies show how the opinions of the audience, divided at first, may eventually come into harmony with the views of the elders hearing a case so as to produce a consensus accepted by all, including the liti-

35. Presumably each litigant contributes one measure of gold. Although there are no clear parallels for such a prize, it is plausible that when the settlement of disputes becomes a time-consuming occupation (cf. Deioces' refusal to continue neglecting his own affairs), litigants should be required to give a gift, in effect a fee, to the judge for settling their dispute.

gants,[36] and the scene on Achilles' shield seems consistent with such a procedure. Whether the litigants themselves or the crowd choose the straightest *dikē*, the settlement is likely to be acceptable to both parties and to the public. Acceptance by everyone, moreover, greatly increases the likelihood of both litigants adhering to the settlement. Thus the litigants in this scene have a dispute they cannot settle themselves. They bring it to a public forum in the hope of finding an arbiter[37] who will give them an acceptable settlement, and they are willing to pay two talents of gold to the man who can do this. Each elder in turn takes the scepter and proposes a solution until, with the approval of the attending crowd, someone finally speaks a settlement acceptable to all, and the one who speaks this settlement receives the two talents of gold.

Perhaps the most disputed point in the scene concerns the precise substance of the dispute. A literal translation of the first lines (498 – 500) runs as follows: "Two men were quarreling about blood-money for a man who had been killed. The one claimed to have

36.
Tiv litigants would seem to believe that the proper and correct solution of a dispute "exists". It "is". The task of the judges is to find it. In the old days the principal litigants would go from one elder of the community to another until they discovered one who could penetrate the details of the case and emerge with this "correct" solution. To a lesser extent, they still do so today. It is obvious to Tiv that when a right decision has been reached, both litigants will concur in it, even though the particular judgment may not be wholly in favor of either. . . . Concurrence of the litigants never occurs without concurrence of the entire community: no one is ready to make concessions while any portion of public opinion still supports him. It is the opinion of the community which forces concurrence. Judging, like all other activities of Tiv leaders, consists largely in the timely suggestion of what the majority thinks is right or desirable. (Bohannan 1957, 64–65)

Cf. the slightly different situation among the Barotse, where several judges deliver their opinions. Here the final judge's verdict is authoritative, even if in rare cases it goes against the others (Gluckman 1955, 15 and 235). On the community's role in dispute settlement see also Humphreys 1983, 230–31.

37. The word *histōr* ("arbiter") is apparently derived from a root meaning "see, know." It designates not one who knows a particular fact but one who has the general wisdom to settle disputes. It occurs once otherwise in Homer, when Idomeneus and Ajax disagree about who is in first place in the chariot race (*Il.* 23.450–98). Idomeneus proposes that they make a wager on the outcome and appoint Agamemnon as *histōr*. Presumably Agamemnon would decide the outcome of the race if they could not decide it themselves. See further Wolff 1946, 37–40.

paid all, demonstrating [his case] to the people, but the other refused to accept anything."[38] As this translation indicates, the Greek text suggests that there are two different points at issue: first whether or not the blood-money has in fact been paid, and second whether or not blood-money must be accepted. Almost all scholars have maintained that one or the other of these is the sole point of the dispute, and many translations have been adjusted to remove the apparent discrepancy. It is likely, however, that the real issue is not so simple as either of these views suggests.

The main objection to the view that the dispute concerns whether or not money has been paid is that the payment required in a homicide case must have amounted to a substantial quantity of goods, and such a payment would almost certainly have been made in front of witnesses. Thus it seems likely that the simple fact of whether or not the payment had been made could easily be determined by a court and that no litigant, therefore, could hope to gain the court's support for a false claim to have paid. As has recently been noted,[39] moreover, the wide gap between the two sides (all vs. nothing) would make it especially easy to determine which litigant is lying, if it were merely a question of fact. On the other hand, if one party (presumably a relative of the dead man) really did not want to accept blood-money, it also seems unlikely that he would voluntarily submit the dispute to a trial at which he might be forced to do so. The regular result of a homicide in Homer is that the killer is pursued into exile,[40] and the relatives of homicide victims seldom seem ready even to consider a settlement. In view of this common standard of behavior throughout the poem, it seems doubtful that a victim's relatives could somehow be forced to accept blood-money at this time.

It is thus likely that the issue is more complex than either of these views. I have elsewhere suggested the possibility of some disagreement among the relatives of the victim: perhaps one of them has accepted blood-money but another one does not wish to accept anything, and hence a dispute arises between the uncompromising relative and the killer.[41] Another possibility is that the litigants are

38.   δύο δ' ἄνδρες ἐνείκεον εἵνεκα ποινῆς
      ἀνδρὸς ἀποφθιμένου· ὁ μὲν εὔχετο πάντ' ἀποδοῦναι
      δήμῳ πιφαύσκων, ὁ δ' ἀναίνετο μηδὲν ἑλέσθαι.
39. Anderson 1976, 13.
40. See Gagarin 1981a, 6–10.
41. Ibid., 13–16.

really engaged in bargaining about the amount of blood-money acceptable to the relatives; the killer has already paid (or deposited with a third party) the amount normally paid in such cases, but the relatives think this is not enough and are seeking a larger payment. The relatives adopt as a bargaining position a refusal to accept anything, and the two parties' inability to agree on a sum forces them to resort to others for a settlement of their dispute.

There are undoubtedly other possible explanations, but in any case I suspect the brief statements presented by the poet only hint at the full complexity of the case. The important fact for our purpose, however, is the description of a procedure that is public and formal and that in several important respects (voluntary submission of the dispute to figures of authority, persuasiveness of the final verdict) fits the picture of early dispute settlement already drawn from the evidence of Herodotus and Hesiod. There are differences, of course, in the grouping of judges into a body and the selection of a final settlement from one of them, but these variations do not constitute a separate procedure.

Homer gives us another brief glimpse of this legal process in preliterate Greece in the underworld scene in the *Odyssey* (11.568–71), where Odysseus sees Minos, "seated, holding a golden *skēptron* and giving judgments to the dead; and they were asking him, their lord, for settlements (*dikas*), seated and standing throughout the wide-gated house of Hades."[42] Here only one judge is mentioned and the litigants do not appear to have any choice among judges, but are forced to crowd around Minos. In important respects, however, the procedure is similar to that in the scene on Achilles' shield. Litigants, apparently voluntarily, bring their disputes to a recognized place for settlement by a scepter-holding, authoritative judge, around whom a crowd is gathered. We do not know the nature of these disputes (they presumably did not include homicide cases), but the scene is further confirmation of the existence of a public, formal procedure for settling disputes at this time.

The dispute between Odysseus and Ajax for the arms of Achilles, briefly mentioned in the *Odyssey* (11.543–51), apparently followed a similar pattern. Odysseus (and presumably Ajax too) presented

42. ἔνθ' ἦ τοι Μίνωα ἴδον, Διὸς ἀγλαὸν υἱόν,
χρύσεον σκῆπτρον ἔχοντα, θεμιστεύοντα νέκυσσιν,
ἥμενον· οἱ δέ μιν ἀμφὶ δίκας εἴροντο ἄνακτα,
ἥμενοι ἑσταότες τε, κατ' εὐρυπυλὲς "Αϊδος δῶ.

his case to Athena and the "sons of the Trojans," who judged it.[43] There are hints in the later tradition of unfair play and Ajax's suicide shows that he certainly did not accept the settlement, which in this case was a victory for Odysseus rather than a compromise. But it does appear that they both submitted their dispute to a supposedly impartial judge, and to this extent they were adhering to the traditional procedure we have described.

Hesiod's dispute with his brother Perses, as presented in the *Works and Days* (27–39), also appears consistent with this picture of dispute settlement.[44] The dispute arose, we are told, after the two brothers had divided their inheritance (37). Now the "kings" (either individually or perhaps in a body) have indicated a willingness to pronounce a settlement (*dikē*, 39)[45] but this has apparently not ended the dispute, since Hesiod pleads with Perses that they should settle it themselves on the spot with straight *dikai* (35–36). Hesiod may fear that the settlement that will be proposed by the kings will not be straight enough (in other words, will not be acceptable to him) or he may simply not want to spend any more on court fees for the "gift-devouring kings." In either case he is urging Perses to work out a settlement without resorting to the help of the kings.[46]

It seems clear that Perses cannot compel Hesiod to accept what-

43. Odysseus sees the ghost of Ajax, "angered over the victory which I won, pleading my case by the ships" (κεχολωμένη εἵνεκα νίκης,/τήν μιν ἐγὼ νίκησα δικαζόμενος παρὰ νηυσί, 11.544–45); the sons of the Trojans and Pallas Athena "judged" the case (δίκασαν, 11.547). The Trojan prisoners were presumably selected as judges because they would be less biased than any Greek. For the sense of *dikazein* here, see Talamanca 1979, 108–9.

44. I am assuming there actually was a dispute and that the details, however vague, given by Hesiod are reasonably accurate. Even if the dispute is entirely a poetic fiction, however (as suggested by Griffith 1983, 57), Hesiod is likely to have drawn a picture of the process for settling disputes with details familiar to his audience.

45. The force of τήνδε δίκην ἐθέλουσι δικάσσαι (39) is disputed. If the words are translated "see fit to make this their judgment," implying that the kings have already proposed a specific settlement, as West argues (1978, ad loc.), then the content of this settlement "has to be inferred from the context," which seems to me very difficult. More suited to the context, and an equally possible interpretation of the Greek, is that the kings "are willing to settle this case" (see Gagarin 1974, 108, n. 13). If this interpretation is correct, it is still possible, and indeed likely, that the kings have already indicated, at least in general terms, the kind of settlement they will propose, which may be a reason for Hesiod's desire to settle out of court.

46. The middle voice, διακρινώμεθα (35), could possibly mean "let us get our quarrel settled" (i.e., by the kings), but αὖθι ("on the spot") implies that Hesiod wants to settle the dispute by themselves rather than taking it to someone else.

ever settlement might be (or might have been) proposed by the kings, and we must thus conclude that any settlement must be accepted by both parties.[47] The pressure of public opinion may also be a factor in this case, and some scholars have felt that the recital of the *Works and Days* was an attempt to marshal this opinion, but the use of a formal, public procedure, whereby a settlement is obtained from the kings, must still be a voluntary step by both parties. And of course the existence of an established system of judicial procedure, controlled by the kings, is presupposed by Hesiod's remarks.

The voluntary nature of judicial procedure is also apparent in the story of Sisyphus's dispute with Aithon as told in the now lost poem *Catalogue of Women* (frag. 43a.31−57), traditionally attributed to Hesiod.[48] Despite the fragmentary state of the papyrus remains of this poem, the general outlines of the story are clear. Sisyphus pays (or perhaps agrees to pay) Aithon a large price, including many cattle, for his daughter, Mestra. After he has taken Mestra away to be his son's bride, she escapes and returns to her father's house.[49] Sisyphus demands that either Mestra or his cattle be returned, but Aithon refuses (he may have already consumed the cattle to sate his immense hunger). The poem continues (36−40):

> And straightaway strife and a dispute arose between Sisyphus and Aithon over the slim-ankled girl. No mortal was able to judge the case, and so they referred it to [a goddess, probably Athena] and they approved her. And she unerringly settled the matter and [spoke a straight?] settlement.[50]

47. In his brief discussion of this passage MacDowell (1978, 14−16) says, "a man who considers himself unfairly treated by another can appeal to the king, and the king gives his decision" (15), which is binding on both parties. I do not find support for this view in Hesiod's text. For a fuller discussion of the question of compulsory trial and sentence with regard to this passage, see Wolff 1946, 59−62.

48. West (1985, 130−37) dates the *Catalogue* to between 580 and 520. Janko (1982, 85−87) suggests a date rather near that of the *Theogony* (early seventh century). There is general agreement that the *Catalogue* is not Hesiod's work.

49. Aithon apparently made a practice of selling his daughter for a large price and then having her escape and return to him to be sold again; see the scholium on Lycophron 1393 (Merkelbach and West 1967, frag. 43b).

50. αἶ]ψα [δ᾽ ἄ]ρ᾽ ἀ[λλ]ήλοισ[ι]ν ἔρις καὶ ν[εῖκος] ἐτ[ύχθη
   Σισύφωι ἠδ᾽ Αἴθωνι τανισφύρο[υ εἵ]νεκα [κούρης,
   ο]ὐδ᾽ ἄρα τις δικάσαι [δύ]νατο βροτός· ἀλλ᾽ αραπ[
   ...... ἐπ]έτρεψαν καὶ ἐπήινεσαν· ἡ δ᾽ ἄρα τοῖ[σιν
   ἀ]τρεκέως διέθηκ[ε] δίκην δ.[

Kakridis (1975, 21−22) suggests that Mestra herself judges the dispute, but this

The precise wording of the goddess's remarks is uncertain, but she apparently declares a general rule to the effect that "when one wishes to recover the price one has paid for something" [without giving up the object], one must lose both the object and the payment, "for once payment is made, it cannot be reclaimed" (41–43).[51] The actual terms of the final settlement are also unclear, though Sisyphus apparently does not get either Mestra or his cattle back.[52] Whatever the settlement, it is clear that the two disputants refer their case voluntarily to a third party for settlement, that both parties approve the choice of this arbitrator, and that she is a figure of some authority (apparently not a mortal). Although the process does not appear to be as formal or as public as in the other cases we have examined, the disputants are clearly adhering to the established procedure for submitting their dispute for settlement.

Further evidence for this procedure can also be found in several disputes in Homer that are not settled by third parties but that nonetheless reflect certain features of formal judicial procedure. Let us first consider the dispute between Menelaus and Antilochus after the chariot race in Book 23 of the *Iliad*, which is settled informally by the two disputants themselves, but in a public forum. The dis-

---

seems unlikely. In Greek literature the object of a dispute settles the dispute only (to my knowledge) in cases where two or more suitors seek the hand of the same woman. The present case is quite different.

51.   ε]ὖτέ τις ἀντ᾽ ὤνοιο χατίζηι χ[ρῆ]μ᾽ ἀνελ[έσθαι,

      ἀ]μφὶ μάλα χρῆν ὤν[ον.......]. τῖμον [

      οὐ γ]ὰρ δὴ μεταμειπ[τόν, ἐπὴν τά] πρῶτ᾽ [ἀποδώηι.

It is interesting to note that the settlement here is apparently delivered in the form of a general conditional sentence (with εὖτε for εἰ), supported by an even more general principle. This may provide a clue to the form of some early Greek legal settlements; cf. Gagarin 1981b, 77. West (1963, 754 and 1985, 169) suggests that Athena's judgment is the *aition* for an actual Athenian law. It is not impossible that there is some reference here to a law of Solon, but it seems equally possible that the allusion is to a general (unwritten) rule.

52. Merkelbach's view of the settlement (Merkelbach 1968) is that Sisyphus seeks the return of his cattle and is denied them according to the rule that once a sale is completed it is irrevocable. But it seems unlikely that Sisyphus would not then insist on the return of Mestra herself. Kakridis 1975 has proposed a more complex and largely speculative interpretation of the situation, that Sisyphus was trying to use Mestra for the same purpose as Aithon was, namely cheating others out of a sale, and so he rightly loses both her and his cattle. West (1963, 754–55) maintains that Sisyphus keeps his cattle, which he had pledged but had not yet delivered, and also receives some mules from Aithon as a result of the settlement. I see no way to decide this matter, given the fragmentary state of the text.

pute arises out of the events of the race: Menelaus has the faster
horses, but Antilochus manages in a bold maneuver to pass him in a
narrow stretch when Menelaus, fearing a crash, slackens his horses
for a moment.[53] Antilochus finishes just ahead of Menelaus, and in
the presence of the assembled Achaeans he claims the second prize
(a mare) after Diomedes, who came in first. Achilles is about to give
it to him when Menelaus rises, takes the *skēptron* and states his
case: "Antilochus, you have dishonored my *aretē* and impeded my
horses, putting your own inferior horses ahead of mine" (571–72).
Menelaus asks the others for a fair settlement,[54] but then without
waiting he himself proposes a "straight" settlement (*itheia*, 580),
namely that Antilochus should swear a formal oath by Poseidon
"that you did not intentionally constrain my chariot with a trick"
(585).[55]

Antilochus ignores the request for an oath and instead answers
with a subtle speech, deferring to Menelaus's superior status and
blaming his own youthful shortcomings for the quarrel between
them, while at the same time implicitly denying any specific wrongdoing and claiming that the prize is truly his (587–95): "Restrain
yourself, for I am much younger than you, Lord Menelaus, and you
are my superior and the better man. You know what excesses (*hy-
perbasiai*) are characteristic of a young man, whose mind is quick
but whose skill (*mētis*) is slight. Bear with me in your heart; I my-

53. Although there is some ambiguity in the poet's description of the method by
which Menelaus is overtaken, by reading the description of the race in the light of
Nestor's earlier advice to Antilochus (23.306–48) we can reconstruct the action as
follows (for the details see Gagarin 1983): as they approach the turn, Menelaus
moves over to try to prevent Antilochus from passing where the road narrows, since
he feels Antilochus should wait until the track broadens again (422–27). Antilochus
then goes off the road (423–34), turns tightly, and forces Menelaus to draw back or
risk a collision in the narrow stretch (429–37). There appears to be no clear rule
governing the situation. The competitive urge to win (widely recognized in Greece as
a good thing) leads to a tactic that is unorthodox (and therefore frowned upon by
some) but not clearly unethical or "illegal."

54. Menelaus's exact words, "settle this case in the open for both of us, not to the
advantage of either" (ἐς μέσον ἀμφοτέροισι δικάσσατε, μηδ᾽ ἐπ᾽ ἀρωγῇ, 23.574),
indicate that a compromise settlement is sought, and suggest that a "straight" *dikē*
(23.580) is one that divides the claims of the two parties evenly. Thür notes (1970,
430) that it makes no sense to divide the mare literally in half, but this hardly pre-
cludes the reaching of a compromise settlement.

55. Menelaus seems to imply that if Antilochus swears this oath, he can keep the
mare. It is doubtful, however, whether Menelaus would really let the matter rest if
Antilochus were to swear an oath that, in Menelaus's view at least, would be false.

self shall give you the mare, which I have won, and if you should ask for anything more from my possessions, I should prefer to give it to you immediately than to fall from favor with you, Zeus-nourished, for all time and be wrong in the eyes of the gods." The speech is so effective[56] that when Antilochus gives him the mare, Menelaus relents and gives her back, "though she is mine," as he says (610). Thus in the end Antilochus has the mare and Menelaus takes the third prize, a cauldron. Both men appear quite satisfied with the final settlement.[57]

The dispute here is settled by the parties themselves, not by a judge, though Menelaus is ready to submit the dispute to others if he and Antilochus cannot settle it themselves. Even though the settlement here is informal, it shows the same tendency toward compromise we noted above. We should also note the use of the scepter, which here too is a symbol of judicial authority, and the request for an oath, for which we shall see more evidence later. And though scholars often assume that Antilochus is in the wrong and has clearly violated the established rules, a close examination of Homer's description of the race shows that his claim to the prize has considerable validity. Of course Menelaus feels he has been cheated, since his horses are faster, but Antilochus comes in ahead, as the poet tells us, "by his skill, not by the speed of his horses" (23.515), just as Nestor had advised him. Thus both parties have a partially valid claim to the prize and must find a compromise settlement.

In contrast to the cases we have thus far examined, neither of the principal disputes in the Homeric poems is settled by a judicial process. The quarrel between Agamemnon and Achilles is eventually

56. Antilochus makes two other similarly effective speeches during the funeral games. First, just before his dispute with Menelaus, he objects (23.543–54) to Achilles' proposal to award second prize to Eumelus, who came in last but would have been first or second if Athena had not caused him to have an "accident." Antilochus threatens to fight for the mare and then proposes a settlement (*dikē*, 23.542), that Eumelus receive a special prize instead. (Primmer 1970, 5–6 and others stress that Antilochus's threat here is an example of an early process of self-help, but neglect to mention the compromise settlement he also proposes.) Achilles accepts this proposal, allowing Antilochus to claim the prize for second place. Later, after coming in last in the footrace, Antilochus briefly praises the other contestants and adds a word of special praise for Achilles (23.787–92), who then adds half a talent of gold to his prize.

57. The compromise solution that defuses a potential dispute between Antilochus and Eumelus (see preceding note) results similarly in the satisfaction of both parties.

settled primarily because of changes in Achilles' emotional state brought on by other events (particularly the death of Patroclus), and Odysseus's dispute with the suitors is, of course, settled by force. In both cases, however, there are attempts to settle the dispute peacefully, and these also reflect the same basic elements of judicial procedure.

In the *Iliad* there are two unsuccessful attempts to find a settlement acceptable to both sides.[58] In Book 1 Nestor proposes a compromise, asking each disputant to back down, but both refuse. In Book 9 Agamemnon himself, under Nestor's prodding, proposes a settlement he thinks will be acceptable to Achilles, who, however, rejects it at this time. In Agamemnon's proposed settlement, which Achilles does accept later, the material restitution that is offered is of substantially greater value than the loss Achilles suffered, but these gifts are relatively insignificant in achieving the final settlement (see *Iliad* 19.146–48), which depends on Achilles giving up his wrath and rejoining the Greek forces under the command of Agamemnon. In terms of the emotional need for recognition and honor, Agamemnon's proposed settlement and the final settlement are compromises in which Achilles' prowess is recognized but is enlisted in the aid of Agamemnon's campaign.

In the *Odyssey*, after Odysseus has killed Antinous and identified himself to the other suitors, one of their leaders, Eurymachus, proposes a peaceful settlement (22.54–59): in exchange for their lives the suitors will restore the property they have devoured by giving Odysseus the equivalent of twenty cattle each. Odysseus immediately rejects this proposal and proceeds to slaughter the suitors. The proposals of Nestor and Eurymachus fail, but they both illustrate the means by which a dispute might be settled when conditions are more favorable or when one or both litigants are more amenable to pressure from others. All the settlements proposed, moreover, including the settlement finally reached in the *Iliad*, are compromises of the kind we would expect to result from a formal

58. One should note that although Agamemnon is probably to be seen as the primary cause of the dispute, since he makes the initial mistake of refusing to allow Chryses to ransom his daughter (in which case he would have received adequate compensation for her loss), Achilles is also partly to blame for it. Indeed, Agamemnon is ready to defer and perhaps abandon his request for a slave-girl to replace the one he is giving up (1.140), when Achilles delivers a harsh and aggressive challenge to his leadership, vowing to leave the fighting and return home (1.149–71). Only then does Agamemnon decide to take Briseis.

settlement and involve restitution for that which one party has taken from the other.

The evidence for legal procedure in Homer, Hesiod and the *Catalogue of Women* can be supplemented by examining two other disputes found in later works. Although both occur in works composed after the earliest enactment of written laws, they clearly reflect the same formal public procedure we have seen in the earlier works. The first is the dispute between Hermes and Apollo in the Homeric *Hymn to Hermes*.[59] This conflict arises when, on the day of his birth, Hermes steals Apollo's cattle, hides them in a cave, and slaughters two of them. He then returns home, tucks himself in his cradle, and makes himself appear the picture of innocence. His mother scolds him for his behavior, but he replies that he is seeking the best means to insure them wealth and honor for the future. When Apollo comes the next day to inquire about his cattle, Hermes denies everything and swears an oath that he is innocent, claiming not even to know what cattle are. The dispute threatens to become violent, as Apollo seizes Hermes and begins to carry him off, but Hermes then suggests that they go to Zeus for a settlement (312). The two continue their dispute, but as they match each other trick for trick, Hermes slowly leads the way to Mount Olympus. Here lie the "scales of justice" (324), and the gods are gathered in assembly (326).[60]

Apollo speaks first, accusing Hermes of the theft of his cattle (334–64). Hermes responds with a counteraccusation that Apollo entered his house in an illegal search (368–86).[61] He then declares (truly) that he did not drive the cattle to his house, and swears an oath to that effect. He ends with a plea for Zeus's help. Zeus immediately sees through Hermes' story, and is in fact amused at how skillfully he has denied Apollo's accusation. He then bids them both make up their differences (391) and tells Hermes to lead Apollo to his cattle. They quickly find the hidden cattle but do not yet end their dispute, since Apollo has no compensation for his two slaughtered animals. But Hermes softens Apollo's anger by playing his

59. Janko (1982, 140–43) dates the *Hymn to Hermes* to the close of the sixth century.

60. Whatever the original reading at the beginning of line 325, it is clear that the gods have gathered in a formal assembly (ὁμήγυριν, 332).

61. Hermes' complaint against Apollo may have been valid, since in classical Athens, at any rate, one was not allowed to enter another's house to search for stolen goods without observing certain formalities; see MacDowell 1978, 148.

newly invented lyre, and Apollo, pleased with the music, says, "I think we shall soon settle our dispute peacefully" (438). Hermes then gives Apollo the lyre, and in return Apollo makes him the herdsman for his flocks. They return to Olympus, swear oaths of friendship, and are firm friends ever after.

We should note that although Hermes has clearly done injury to Apollo and is caught manifestly telling a misleading (though not entirely false) story, Zeus prescribes no punishment for him. Indeed he proposes no explicit settlement at all, though he does indicate that any settlement they reach themselves (which would presumably be a compromise) should include Apollo's recovering his cattle. Instead of outrage, moreover, Zeus expresses amusement at Hermes' skill in lying. It appears that Hermes' actions are blameworthy in that stealing the cattle and lying about it are in some way reprehensible, but they are also praiseworthy in that he does both with extraordinary skill.[62] Hermes must be aware that he has done Apollo injury, but he feels (apparently rightly, as it turns out) that only by these unusual means can he eventually gain the recognition and honor he desires and does in fact acquire (cf. 166–81). Thus the position of each party has a certain validity, and they agree to submit the dispute to a higher authority in a formal, public setting. They are not actually given a settlement by Zeus, but with the help of this procedure they are able by themselves to reach a compromise settlement.

Finally, let us consider briefly the trial of Orestes in Aeschylus's *Eumenides*. This work is later (458 B.C.) than the others we have thus far examined and the trial is more formal; unlike the earlier proceedings it ends with a clear verdict by the court in favor of one party, Orestes. If we consider not merely the trial and verdict, however, but the procedure as a whole, we find several of the same features as the procedures pictured in the earlier works.

---

62. Cf. Bohannan:

Tiv hold two conflicting notions about thieves and stealing. They say that Tiv are the best thieves in the world, and that a good thief is one who can break through the mud wall of a hut, enter, and take out all the contents, including a bicycle, without waking the sleeping occupants. They admire the technical skill of any thief who can come close to this achievement. . . . At the same time, Tiv say that stealing is an *ifer* ("crime") and cannot be allowed to go unpunished. The usual way of punishing a thief is to beat him and take back one's goods. (1957, 124)

Cf. Burkert on Hermes and cattle rustling: "In this context [the herdsman's life] cattle rustling is unquestionably a virtue, as long as it remains undetected" (1985, 158).

First, both parties voluntarily agree to submit the dispute to Athena's judgment. Orestes puts himself under her protection and says he will await the outcome of his case (235–43), and though the Furies attack him, in their first confrontation with Athena they ask her to give them a straight settlement (*dikē*) of the issue, and they put the outcome in her hands (433–35).[63] The reason both parties ask for a settlement is, of course, that each feels its own case is valid. Neither party disputes the fact that Orestes killed Clytemnestra, but each gives this fact a different legal interpretation.

Second, though the verdict of the court releases Orestes from the Furies' pursuit, it does not entirely settle the dispute. The Furies threaten further violence and must in the end be reconciled through a compromise that awards them an honor corresponding to the honor of Orestes' acquittal. Athena as judge can only partially impose her verdict; for a full settlement she must work out a compromise between the two disputants and the forces they represent. Only when she has persuaded the Furies to accept this compromise, give up their wrath, and join as partners in the new prosperity of Athens can the dispute truly be said to be settled.

Third, we should note that the Furies have apparently asked Orestes to swear an oath denying he killed his mother, which he has refused to do (429).[64] In sum, despite the presence of a more formal trial procedure in this later work, the dispute between Orestes and the Furies, like the earlier disputes, is voluntarily submitted to a judge for settlement and is in the end settled by a compromise acceptable to both sides.

From all this evidence a fairly full picture of the process of settling disputes in early Greece can be drawn. The main elements of this procedure are (1) the dispute is voluntarily submitted to a

63. It is misleading to describe this process as Wolff does: "It is Orestes, the defendant, who calls on Athena in order to obtain a trial that he hopes will rid him of his torturers. . . . Athena thereupon, with the consent of the parties, . . . arranges the trial" (1946, 47). But the Furies too, without any prompting, ask Athena to hear the case (431–35), and only then does she arrange for a trial.

64. The Furies say that Orestes "neither accepts nor is willing to give an oath" [ἀλλ' ὅρκον οὐ δέξαιτ' ἄν, οὐ δοῦναι θέλει, 429]. They refer to the fact that even if one did not agree to swear an oath offered by the other party, one could offer an oath oneself for one's opponent to swear. Cf. Antiphon ("the Sophist") frag. 44A, col. 5.8–14 and Aristotle, *Rhetoric* 1377A8–29, where the tendering and accepting of oaths is clearly seen as a rhetorical strategy. There is no indication in *Eumenides* that if Orestes did swear an oath, the Furies would immediately cease their pursuit.

scepter-holding judge or group of judges for settlement; (2) each disputant claims to have, and to some extent does have, a valid case; (3) a solution involving some compromise and acceptable to both sides is found or proposed; (4) the settlement is proposed and accepted (if it is accepted) in a public place, such as the agora or an assembly; [65] (5) public opinion may be a factor in persuading the parties to submit their dispute for settlement; (6) an oath of denial may be sworn or asked for by one of the parties, though this oath does not necessarily settle the case; [66] (7) when a dispute arises out of someone's loss of property, a settlement should lead to the restoration of that property, either in full or in large part; and finally, (8) in addition to a property settlement the acknowledgment of each disputant's honor is a factor in several settlements. Injured pride is at least as powerful a factor as material damages in many disputes.

Perhaps the most significant variation in these cases is in the number of judges. Deioces was at first only one of several judges available to the people; Minos is apparently the only judge present among the dead; [67] on Achilles' shield a body of judges is assembled, though each proposes his own settlement; and the jury in *Eumenides* votes on the verdict. In other cases (such as Hesiod) more than one judge is mentioned but we cannot tell whether they carried out their duties separately or in a body. Clearly the judicial function is related to kingship; the scepter is an essential token of both judge and king. [68] But since the scepter is often wielded by heralds and others, as well as by kings, and since the word *basileus* ("king") is often

65. On the importance of the public forum for Homeric justice, see Havelock 1978, esp. chaps. 7–8.

66. Latte (1920, 5–47) surveys the evidence for a variety of oaths in Greek legal procedure. He rightly stresses the voluntary nature of the submission of disputes but (in my view) goes too far in minimizing the role of the judge in early procedure. Gernet (1968, 241–47) sees this sacred oath as a survival of the earliest religious formulas of legal procedure, whereby guilt or innocence was immediately and automatically established rather than being judged (cf. Thür 1970). It is possible that oaths once did have this function, but in the surviving evidence they do not. Antilochus sidesteps the oath that is offered him; Hermes swears a more-or-less false oath, which certainly does not decide the case, and Orestes refuses to swear the oath offered him but is acquitted anyway. In the judicial procedure of some societies evidentiary oaths may be used to settle straightforward questions of fact, but they are of little help in the more complex disputes we find portrayed in early Greek literature.

67. In later tradition Minos's brother, Rhadamanthys, was also a noted judge among the dead, but he is not mentioned as such in Homer.

68. See n. 28 above.

applied rather broadly to a number of distinguished members of a community,[69] it is possible that the judicial function was never in fact restricted to only one person in a community.[70] Thus in the standard procedure it is likely that several judges are potentially available who might render a settlement to the litigants, but the actual settlement is rendered by a single judge.

Even when the judges were assembled as a body, the decision to submit a dispute for settlement was voluntary. It is worth emphasizing that the evidence for the voluntary submission of disputes is overwhelming. The story of Deioces, Hesiod's description of the Muses' assisting a king, the scene on the shield of Achilles, and the disputes between Hesiod and Perses, Sisyphus and Aithon, Hermes and Apollo, and Orestes and the Furies all point to the conclusion that disputes were submitted for settlement on the agreement of both parties.

These examples we have considered[71] are sufficient to establish beyond doubt that there existed in Greece before the introduction of writing a recognized procedure for settling disputes which clearly meets our criteria for a legal procedure, namely that it be public and formal. Even though private, informal settlements are possible, a formal, public procedure is clearly available to those who wish to use it. Only two early examples, the trial on Achilles' shield and the picture of Minos judging the dead, show us the formal procedure in actual operation, but the other cases, even those in which the formal procedure is not used or the proposed settlement is not ac-

69. Calhoun: "The *gerontes* ["elders"] are often called βασιλῆες and in general are accorded the same titles and the same epithets as the king" (1962, 437). In the most recent survey of the word *basileus* in early Greece, Drewes (1983, 98–108) argues that the word has a broader meaning than "king" and translates it as "highborn leader." This conclusion is certainly open to doubt, but it is clear that the word does not necessarily denote a ruler with all the attributes of a "king." See also Geddes 1984, 28–36.

70. Although a single judge (Athena?) is selected by Sisyphus and Aithon to settle their dispute, it is implied that other judges were considered or at least might have been chosen.

71. I have not included the argument between Ajax and Idomeneus (*Il.* 23.450–98; see n. 37 above) in this list, since I do not think it ever truly becomes a dispute; but cf. MacDowell 1978, 13–14 and Cantarella 1979, 215–21. Nor have I mentioned the dispute (*stasis*) which arose among the Achaeans after the killing of Thersites by Achilles, as told in the *Aethiopis*, since we are given no information concerning the nature of the dispute or its settlement except that Achilles went to Lesbos and was cleansed of the homicide (Proclus, *Chrest.* 2; see p. 14, n. 43, above).

cepted, confirm the existence of the procedure as well as the details summarized above. Indeed the procedure is sufficiently familiar to Homer's audience that when Odysseus recounts his long wait for Charybdis to disgorge the remains of his shattered ship, he says, "at the time when a man rises to go to dinner from [sitting in] the agora judging many quarrels of young men who submit them," [72] then the timbers of the ship appeared. The details of this image of a man sitting until late in the day in the agora judging cases are completely consistent with the picture we have drawn from the other evidence, and its use as a simile in this context confirms the familiarity of the scene.

The procedure appears to be used primarily for disputes arising out of conflicting claims, often involving the honor or *aretē* of the disputants. Alleged violations of specific rules are often a factor in the dispute, but other rules or extenuating circumstances are also involved, so that the alleged violator has some justification for his actions. Simple violations of rules are treated outside the legal process, as, for example, Odysseus's punishment of the suitors. [73] Although submission of a dispute for settlement is voluntary on both sides, it is likely that public pressure could be brought to bear on a reluctant disputant. The more powerful members of the society were naturally less susceptible to this pressure, and disputes involving them were less likely to be settled by means of this legal process. Nonetheless, a formal, public procedure was clearly available and must have been used regularly by the common people during this proto-legal stage of social development.

One final characteristic of this procedure should be noted. Although it follows well-established patterns, we do not find the strict formal requirements for procedure often found in other early legal systems. There is no evidence of special formulas or obscure rules for presenting a case and no persons specially trained in the technical intricacies of procedure, as there were, for example, in early Iceland. Oratorical skill and the shrewd art of tactful compromise are clearly important in the Greek examples, but the procedure ap-

---

72. ἦμος δ' ἐπὶ δόρπον ἀνὴρ ἀγορῆθεν ἀνέστη / κρίνων νείκεα πολλὰ δικαζομένων αἰζηῶν (*Od.* 12.439–40). The use of *anēr* ("man") does not mean (*pace* Talamanca 1979, 107–8) that this judge is to be differentiated from the *basileis* or *gerontes* normally named.

73. Note, however, that even in this case the suitors have a certain justification for their behavior; see esp. *Od.* 24.121–90.

pears to be available to all full members of the society on an equal basis. Even at this stage we see some of the openness and publicness so characteristic of legal procedure in classical Athens, and apparently in Greek law in general. To be sure, any such picture based on literary evidence alone is likely to be idealized; and yet the details are consistent enough from case to case that the picture must be based on actual conditions.

We can also see in this early literature a growing recognition of the importance of judicial procedure for the well-being of a peaceful society. The value of legal procedure is clearly recognized in the fifth-century works we have discussed, Aeschylus's *Eumenides* and Herodotus's story of Deioces. It is also indicated by the presence of the trial scene in the portrayal on Achilles' shield of the city at peace, characterized only by marriage processions and the trial. The city at peace is contrasted not only with the city at war (18.509−40), which exemplifies the failure to settle disputes peacefully, but also with the rural scenes that follow (541−606). This seems to imply that a procedure for settling disputes peacefully has become more formalized in the newly developing polis than it was in the traditional rural estates, where the lord of the estate probably settled disputes himself as they arose. The scene suggests a connection between the growth of the polis and the development of more formal judicial procedures, and it is plausible that as the scattered populations of the early dark age came together into larger, more organized settlements, the procedure for settling disputes would become more formal. In the ideal polis, Homer seems to be saying, even an emotion-laden dispute stemming from a homicide ought to be submitted to others for settlement by means of this procedure. The shield of Achilles thus contains the implicit message that judicial procedure is central to the life of the polis.[74]

Hesiod delivers the same message to his audience explicitly. In the passage from the *Theogony* considered above, he implies that settling disputes is one of the primary duties of a king;[75] in his later poem, the *Works and Days*, he devotes a long section to the praise

74. For the connection between the growth of the polis and the development of legal procedure, see chap. 6 below.

75. Cf. Aristotle, *Pol.* 1285B9−12, where after stating that early kings led armies and supervised sacrifices he adds that they also judged cases [τὰς δίκας ἔκρινον], some on oath, sworn with a scepter, and some not.

of *dikē*, a word variously translated as "legal process," "law," or "justice." [76] I have elsewhere objected to the translation "justice" [77] on the ground that this word often implies a systematic moral view backed by some sort of higher sanction, an implication not present in the Greek word. If, however, we restrict our application of the word "justice" to the context of a given social and legal order, [78] we may consider it roughly equivalent to *dikē* as Hesiod uses it here.

In this passage (*WD* 213–85) the basic opposition Hesiod uses as a structure for his plea is between *dikē* and *hybris* ("violence, wrongdoing") or *biē* ("violence"). [79] This opposition has a general aspect, namely the contrast between observing and violating the norms of the society, and a more specific aspect referring to the observation or violation of rules for the proper operation of the legal process. As we shall see, this more specific aspect is Hesiod's primary concern, and in this passage he regularly portrays "just" behavior in terms that invoke a context of legal procedure. [80]

Before considering this passage we should first note that Hesiod has already introduced procedural justice in the context of his dispute with Perses (*WD* 27–39, discussed above), when he pleads for a straight settlement. Procedural justice is also his concern in a brief passage in the description of the fifth age of man (the Iron Age), which precedes the section on *dikē*. In lamenting conditions during the present age of iron Hesiod gloomily predicts even worse to come (*WD* 189–94):

> Settlements will be by force [81] and one man will destroy the city of another. And there will be no appreciation of a man who keeps his oath nor of a just (*dikaios*) man nor of a good man, but they will instead honor the doer of evils and vio-

76. See Gagarin 1973.
77. Gagarin 1976, 12–15.
78. See, e.g., Kelsen 1947, esp. 390–98.
79. *WD* 213–18, 225–47, 274–75; cf. 189–94 and 321–26.
80. See Latte: "So stark dieses Rechtsbewusstsein ist [in the *Works and Days*], es beschränkt sich durchaus auf der Prozess und erwächst für Hesiod aus dem Unrecht, das andere ihm antaten" (1946, 68).
81. χειροδίκαι (189) means literally "hand-settlements" and is echoed by δίκη δ' ἐν χερσί ("justice in one's [own] hands") in 192. The second half of this passage (beginning with δίκη δ' ἐν χερσί) to some extent repeats the message of the first half in different words.

lence. Justice (*dikē*) will be by force and there will be no respect, and the worse man will injure the better man by speaking with crooked words, and he will swear a false oath.[82]

That the justice which will be absent from human society is procedural justice is indicated particularly by reference to oaths and
crooked words, since in Hesiod "straight" and "crooked" regularly
refer to the plea of a litigant or the decision of a judge and thus to
judicial procedure.[83] Oaths, as we have seen, are also a common feature of this procedure. Thus before Hesiod turns to his direct praise
of *dikē*, he has in these two passages (*WD* 27–39 and 189–94) already led his audience to think of justice as a procedure that is of
some importance both for himself and for the community.

Hesiod begins his praise of *dikē* with a general admonition to his
brother Perses to observe *dikē* and shun *hybris* (213–18). He then
warns more specifically (219) that *Horkos* ("Oath") will accom-
pany (i.e., punish) crooked *dikai*,[84] and he draws a sad picture
(220–24) of *dikē* being dragged off by the "gift-devouring" kings
who decide cases with crooked settlements. Thus in the opening
lines of his praise of justice Hesiod's general warning to observe *dikē*
becomes a specific warning against corrupting the legal process.

There follows a contrasting pair of descriptions, first of the city
where *dikē* prevails (225–37), which prospers in every way, and

82. I follow West's text (1978) except in 193, where I retain the ms. reading οὐκ
ἔσται. West's reading (ἐσσεῖται) does not change the meaning of the first part of
192–93 ("justice will be by force"), but he must then understand the text to mean
αἰδὼς ἐν χερσὶ ἐσσεῖται ("respect or decency will be by force"), which seems to me
more difficult than the discrepancy alleged by West (at the end of his note, ad loc.).

83. Hesiod's explicit references to straight or crooked speech are in *WD* 194, 258
(see West 1978, ad loc.), 262, and 263. "Straight" and "crooked" occur in the explicit context of judicial procedure in *Th.* 85–86, *WD* 35–36, 221, 224, 262, and
263, and in contexts implying or strongly suggesting judicial procedure in *WD* 9,
194, 219, 226, 250–51, 258, 264, and frag. 286.2. Otherwise the terms are used
only once in reference to *dikē* in general (*WD* 230), once in a general sense perhaps
referring to judicial procedure ("Zeus straightens the crooked," *WD* 7) and once in
a doubtful restoration in a papyrus (frag. 25.11).

84. The crooked *dikai* punished by Horkos (*WD* 219) must be the pleas of the
litigants, which were accompanied by oaths, and perhaps also the settlements proposed by the kings, who may also have sworn oaths (so West 1978, ad loc.). In classical Athens oaths were sworn by both jurors and litigants, but we do not know for
certain that judges also swore oaths in Hesiod's time.

then of the city where *hybris* prevails (238–47), which suffers every sort of evil, even sometimes as a result of only one man's wrongdoing. At the beginning of these descriptions the observance of *dikē* is specifically linked to judicial activity,[85] but in the rest of this section Hesiod may be referring to proper and improper conduct in a more general sense, including both the observance of norms and the proper use of the legal process.

Hesiod next addresses the kings directly (248–73), warning them of the dire consequences that will follow if they violate *dikē*. Here the poet is clearly concerned with violations of the judicial process, as he warns against crooked *dikai* (250–51)[86] and against scorning *dikē* with crooked speech (258)[87] and predicts that the people will pay for the wrongs of the kings who "slant their settlements, speaking them crookedly" (260–62). The kings should straighten out their words and forget crooked settlements (263–64) in order to prevent the possibility that the less just man might get the larger settlement (270–73). In the last section of this passage Hesiod repeats to Perses his admonition to observe *dikē* (274–75). After noting that *dikē* is a distinctive feature of human societies (276–80), he then again emphasizes specifically the importance of the legal process, contrasting the litigant who pleads "justly" (280–81) and swears a true oath (285) with the one who swears a false oath (282–84). Of course the former prospers, whereas the latter's family is obliterated.

The plea for "justice" in this poem is one of the strongest we have from any Greek author. Certainly Hesiod is urging proper (and peaceful) behavior in general, but whenever he introduces examples of proper or improper behavior, he specifically mentions, or at least implies, behavior associated with judicial procedure, either on the part of litigants pleading their cases or of kings hearing these cases and handing down settlements. For Hesiod the prosperity of the whole society depends on the proper functioning of this legal process. Perhaps partly because of his own legal difficulties he came to

85. "Those who give straight settlements [*dikai*] to foreigners and citizens and do not stray at all from what is just [*dikaion*]" (225–26); cf. Aeschylus, *Suppliants* 701–3 for a similar expression (ξένοισι δίκας διδοῖεν).

86. Again in 250–51 *dikai* is ambiguous between "pleas" and "settlements"; see West 1978, ad loc.

87. In 258 the reference is to the judges' decisions; see West 1978, ad loc.

understand, just as the Medes discovered in Herodotus's story of Deioces, that without an effective legal process the social order will disintegrate.

Hesiod's words suggest a certain first-hand acquaintance with social turmoil, and during the two centuries after he wrote (ca. 700 B.C.) many Greek cities experienced a considerable amount of internal strife. This was also the period when many cities took the decisive step in the development of law, the writing down of laws, and it is possible that these two phenomena are somehow connected. The significant point to note at this stage, however, is that even before the Greeks wrote down laws, they had developed a traditional process for settling disputes and had already begun to recognize the importance of this judicial process for the maintenance of peace and prosperity in their society.

3

EARLY WRITTEN LAWS:
THE LITERARY EVIDENCE

We have seen that by the beginning of the seventh century at the latest a formal, public procedure existed in Greece for the peaceful settlement of disputes. The consistency of the testimony of different authors indicates that this practice was not confined to one or two cities but is likely to have been fairly widespread throughout the Greek world.[1] Moreover, although we have virtually no information about the proto-legal institutions of most Greek cities, there is evidence for the formal settlement of disputes in Athens in the period before that city's earliest written laws. Aristotle tells us that the early *thesmothetai* (literally, "lawgivers") recorded decisions and kept them for judging future disputes, and also that the early archons "had the power to judge disputes on their own authority" and not just hold preliminary hearings.[2] Although Aristotle's reliability in pre-Solonian matters is often doubted, it is generally accepted that some officials did hear cases formally before Draco's appointment as lawgiver in about 620 B.C.[3]

Concerning the next step, the writing down of laws, the ancient evidence is strong and consistent: from about the middle of the seventh century, in widely scattered parts of the Greek world, cities be-

1. Strictly speaking, the early literary evidence probably represents Asia Minor (Homer), Boeotia (Hesiod, *Hymn to Hermes*? [see Janko 1982, 143–50]), and Athens (*Catalogue*? [see West 1985, 168–70], *Eumenides*). It is possible that the Doric areas of the Peloponnesus and Crete had different legal institutions.

2. For the *thesmothetai* see *Ath. Pol.* 3.4 (on which see Gagarin 1981b and contra Rhodes 1981, ad loc.). Ronald Stroud has called my attention to Sandys's accurate description of the full force of ἀναγράψαντες: "to engrave on a tablet and set up in a public place (this is the force of ἀνα-); in brief, 'to record publicly.'" I shall discuss this passage further below. For the early archons, see *Ath. Pol.* 3.5, where the expression is τὰς δίκας αὐτοτελεῖς κρίνειν.

3. Note the apparent offer of a trial in the case of Cylon's conspiracy (see p. 19, n. 3, above).

gan to enact written laws. According to the Greeks themselves the earliest written laws, those of Zaleucus for Epizephyrian Locri (in southern Italy), were traditionally dated to about 662 B.C.,[4] and the first legal inscriptions from Dreros in Crete are now dated tentatively to the middle or second half of the seventh century.[5] We know of written laws from quite a few cities by the beginning of the sixth century, and it is likely that by the middle of the century most large Greek cities had written laws, the most notable exception being Sparta (see below). In this chapter I shall examine the literary evidence for the earliest lawgivers and try to ascertain the general nature of the laws they enacted. In the next chapter I shall look at the inscriptional evidence for early laws.

The literary evidence concerning the early lawgivers is, regrettably, late, relatively meager, sometimes inconsistent, and selective. With few exceptions we have no evidence earlier than the mid-fourth century, two centuries or more after the fact. Many of the earliest lawgivers are scarcely more than names. Where we know more, there are sometimes widely divergent accounts of the lives and works of these figures, especially in the cases of Zaleucus and Charondas of Catana. And finally, as in any such tradition, the reports we have are selective: Aristotle, for example, because of his interest in the best distribution of estates in a polis gives us a relatively large amount of information about the inheritance and property regulations of otherwise unknown figures, and even the fuller accounts of Plutarch or Diodorus are naturally more likely to report those laws which are somehow striking or unusual. In spite of all these difficulties, however, I believe we can obtain a reasonably accurate picture of the kinds of subjects treated by the early lawgivers and of the general nature of the laws they wrote. And when the inscriptional evidence of the next chapter is added, we shall have a foundation on which to base a discussion of the nature and purpose of the written laws of archaic Greece.[6] In particular the substantial surviving fragment of the homicide law of Draco gives us an undistorted glimpse of an actual law by the first lawgiver of Athens.[7]

4. For the traditional date (which is likely to be too early), see Mühl 1928, 457.

5. For the Dreros laws, see Jeffery 1961a, 309–16. She disputes the earlier view that the earliest surviving laws from Gortyn also should be dated to the mid-seventh century.

6. By "archaic Greece" I mean the somewhat arbitrarily limited period from about 800 to 500 B.C. For a recent evaluation of this period, see Snodgrass 1980.

7. *IG* I^3.104 (= *IG* I^2.115), republished by Stroud 1968; see also Gagarin 1981a.

Before going further, we must briefly recall some of our discussion of the term "law" in Chapter 1 and make some distinctions with regard to the use of the term in this context. I argued that it is usually necessary to have an official body of rules, recorded in writing, in order that they be "recognized" (in Hart's sense) as laws, since only by such a criterion of recognition can we distinguish laws from other rules. The traditional reports of early lawgivers, however, do not generally adhere to such a distinction, unless the actual written laws of the past are available (as apparently in the case of Solon), and later writers may designate a number of different kinds of rules by the term *nomos*, which may mean "law," "custom," or "way of behavior." Thus we must be careful to distinguish laws from the large body of other rules also called *nomoi*, and we may do so not only by the fact that laws were written but also by certain general criteria differentiating laws from other rules.

In particular we must first distinguish laws from maxims or general statements concerning moral or social behavior. Written laws are normally recorded by an authorized representative of the polis. Their ultimate function is to provide guidelines for decisions by courts or other public agencies, though they may be applied to activity that does not normally come, but might come, before a court, such as laws concerning marriage or wills. Maxims, on the other hand, though they may be inscribed (as, for example, "Nothing in excess" was inscribed on Apollo's temple at Delphi) and may also influence a judicial decision, do not have the authority or official public sanction of law. They are not officially recognized and thus for our purposes do not qualify as laws. Laws normally take the form of third-person singular conditional sentences and in Greece at least are always written in prose.[8] In contrast, maxims are normally expressed in either a short "gnomic" form suitable for oral repetition[9] or in verse, such as the many lines or groups of lines from

8. Roth's thesis, based on Hesiod's *Theogony* 77–103, that early Greek kings or judges memorized traditional rules, which were preserved in verse (Roth 1976), is rejected above in chap. 2.

9. The original Spartan *rhētra* ("pronouncement") quoted by Plutarch (*Lyc.* 6.2) clearly preserves the mnemonic element of rhythmic repetition of sounds, whatever changes its text may have undergone in transmission. It begins, "having built the temple of Zeus Syllanius and of Athena Syllania, having tribed the tribes and obed the obes, etc." Jeffery (1961b, 145–47) argues plausibly that the language of the *rhētra* is not that of written law, but this does not justify her conclusion that it is a later forgery. It is likely that the *rhētra* was originally an oral pronouncement, not a

Hesiod and the later elegiac and lyric poets, that could easily be (and often were) cited as separate sayings.[10] Moreover, maxims have a tendency to contradict one another, since they are never created systematically; such contradictions do not cause the kind of difficulties that result from contradictions in laws. In fact, it may be useful to have contradictory maxims to apply to different situations.[11]

Second, laws can be characterized by a degree of generality intermediate between maxims (or principles) and decrees. Although the dividing lines between these three categories cannot be fixed and some rules may fall into an intermediate area, we may in general state that maxims (e.g., "Give help to your neighbor when needed so that he will in turn help you")[12] pertain to such a general cate-

---

law; in Forrest's words, we have "the text of an oracle, rather than a law" (1963, 179). Interestingly, the later addition to this *rhētra* (*Lyc.* 6.8) reads like a written law, beginning with the standard conditional clause ("but if . . ."). It is quite possible that the *rhētra* was first transmitted orally but was later written down, thereby attaining the special status of a law, despite the apparent prohibition against written laws (*Lyc.* 13.1–4, see below), and that the additional provision was later enacted as a written law. Plutarch (*Lyc.* 6.7) says that the later addition was "written down beside" the original *rhētra* (παρενέγραψαν), which might suggest that the original was written by the time the addition was enacted. Sparta certainly had written laws by the fourth century, since Lycurgus (*Leoc.* 129) quotes the text of a Spartan law. (I owe these last two observations to Douglas MacDowell.)

10. I suspect that the "laws [*nomoi*] of Charondas," which, according to Athenaeus (619B), were sung in Athens during drinking parties (but see Piccirilli 1981, 7–8 for the proposed emendation of Ἀθήνησι to Κατάνησι), were maxims of this sort. Certainly it is hard to imagine any true law, no matter how gracefully versified, being sung at a party, especially in a city in which it would have no status as a law. It is also possible that these sung *nomoi* (*nomos* can also mean a "tune") were the verses not of Charondas but of another poet incorporating or parodying the actual laws of Charondas (cf. Herondas, *Mimes* 2.46ff.). The story (Plutarch *Sol.* 3.5) that Solon attempted to versify his laws is rightly rejected by Linforth (1919, 214). Passages cited by Willetts (1967, 8, n. 3) for the oral recital and transmission of laws do not provide persuasive evidence for the practice anywhere except at Sparta, which in this regard (as in so many others) was clearly exceptional. Piccirilli (1981) assembles the evidence for sung *nomoi* in Greece and accepts virtually all of it. The matter deserves more consideration than I can devote to it here; let me simply say that Piccirilli's argument depends entirely on late and unreliable evidence and ignores the fact that, with the exception of the Spartan *rhētra*, there is no hint of verse or of "forma ritmica" in any of the actual laws of the period.

11. See, for example, Hesiod's advice that it is a good thing to have only one son, but it is also good to have more than one son (*WD* 376–80). Some English examples: "Haste makes waste" vs. "He who hesitates is lost"; "A penny saved is a penny earned" vs. "Penny wise, pound foolish"; "Out of sight, out of mind" vs. "Absence makes the heart grow fonder."

12. Cf. Hesiod *WD* 349–51.

gory of behavior that they do not provide specific guidance in the settlement of a dispute, though they may be cited as justification for specific behavior. Maxims are often expressed in the second-person singular rather than as third-person conditional sentences; sometimes, as in Hesiod's *Works and Days*, they are put in the form of advice to a specific addressee. At the other extreme, decrees are normally directed at a single, temporally limited situation and affect only a limited number of people. In contrast, laws normally mention a specific kind of activity but generalize the rule to include any act of that kind.[13]

Third, we should distinguish between laws proper and a *politeia*, usually translated "constitution." This distinction, made by Aristotle (*Politics* 2.9), is not absolute, since a *politeia* may be expressed in part or in whole by officially "recognized" (and written) laws, as in the Constitution of the United States. But the term basically designates an institutional structure for the governance of a city, which may be based largely on unwritten traditions rather than written statutes, or may be implied by laws concerning various public officials or bodies, or may be expressed in the unofficial writings of thinkers such as Plato (whose *Politeia* is more commonly known as the *Republic*). In Book 2 of his *Politics* Aristotle is primarily concerned with those who have contributed to constitutional theory or practice (see 2.2.1, 2.9.9 *ad fin.*), and it is only as a kind of afterthought that he adds a brief mention of some early lawgivers who did not establish *politeiai*. In what follows I shall be concerned with those who wrote laws and shall mention constitutional reforms only if these probably took the form of written laws.

Fourth, we should perhaps distinguish at Athens between the laws of Draco, which were the first to be written down[14] and were

13. In the late fifth and fourth centuries Athenians could make roughly these same distinctions between general norms (*nomima*), written laws (*nomoi*), and decrees (*psēphismata*); see nn. 41, 54 below on *nomoi* and *nomima*, and Hansen 1978 on *nomoi* and *psēphismata*. Ostwald (1973) has argued that there is no coherent concept of "unwritten law" (*agraphos nomos*) in classical Greece. The earliest occurrence of the term "unwritten law" is in Sophocles' *Antigone* 454–55 (produced ca. 442 B.C.). Cerri 1979, esp. 33–49 has an interesting discussion of Antigone's speech and other passages employing this term.

14. Aristotle, *Ath. Pol.* 41.2. (I treat this work as Aristotle's, though it may be by a member of his school.) The *axōnes* or rotating wooden blocks were the official place of publication for the laws of Draco and Solon, and they probably remained so until the reorganization of the Athenian laws at the end of the fifth century; see Stroud 1979 and Rhodes 1981, 131–35 for differing views concerning the nature of these *axōnes*.

published on official *axōnes* and the work done by the *thesmothetai* who preceded him. These officials, according to Aristotle (*Athē-naiōn Politeia* 3.4), were selected "in order that they might publicly record *thesmia* and keep them for the deciding of disputes." There is some agreement among scholars that by *thesmia* Aristotle means the results of particular court cases, and I have elsewhere argued[15] that an example of a pre-Draconian *thesmion* survives in the tyranny law cited in Aristotle, *Ath. Pol.* 16.10: "The following are ancestral *thesmia* of the Athenians: if any people establish a tyranny or if anyone assists in establishing a tyranny, he shall be outlawed, both he and his family." This statement implies two stages of transcription. First the *thesmothetai* recorded the *thesmion*, or rule established by a particular case, for their own use in future cases. Then later a law reaffirming this ancestral *thesmion* as a valid Athenian law was publicly enacted (probably by Solon).

The evidence of the tyranny law suggests that at least in one case the *thesmothetai* recorded not the particular judicial decision ("X is to be outlawed for attempted tyranny") but the general rule ("if anyone attempts tyranny . . .") on which they based their decision, and they recorded it in the same third-person conditional form in which Draco would later begin his homicide law.[16] This is an important step toward an officially published set of laws, and it may be that most or all of the other *thesmia* they recorded were, like the tyranny law, later reaffirmed in Attic law. However, since these *thesmia* apparently were not enacted by an authorized legislator for public display but were recorded by the *thesmothetai*, who were primarily judges, for their own use, they do not have quite the same status as the later laws of Draco. We know nothing more about the pre-Draconian *thesmothetai*, but if this admittedly speculative reconstruction of their activity is correct, they made a significant contribution to the development of law during this period.[17]

Fifth, before turning to the lawgivers we should say more about

15. See Gagarin 1981b, and also Hignett 1952, 76–77 and Ostwald 1969, 174–75; cf. Rhodes 1981, 102–3.

16. It is possible that a similar *thesmion* survives in the words of the judge who settles the dispute between Sisyphus and Aithon (Hesiod, frag. 43a.41–43, discussed in chap. 2 above); whatever the precise text, the words are a third-person conditional sentence, beginning "when someone" (εὐτέ τις). It has also been suggested that a *thesmion* is preserved in Athenaeus 235A, but this depends on a doubtful emendation of Wilamowitz; see Schlaifer 1943, 40, n. 11.

17. See further chap 6. below.

the exceptional situation at Sparta, where, according to Plutarch (*Lycurgus* 13.1–4), one of the Lycurgan *rhētras* prohibited the use of written laws.[18] The epigraphical evidence appears to confirm this report,[19] and Sparta in this respect, as in so many others, seems to have resisted a movement common to most other Greek cities. There is no evidence, however, to support the view that Sparta may have preserved a set of "laws" orally without inscribing them. Plutarch here only speaks of a prohibition of written laws, not of any oral collection, and Aristotle indicates that the Ephors judged cases "using their own judgment" (*autognōmones*, *Politics* 1270B30; cf. 1272A39); both authors imply a contrast between written laws and no laws at all rather than between written and oral laws.

As to the nature of unwritten Spartan *nomoi*, an observation attributed to Zeuxidamus is illuminating.[20] Zeuxidamus reportedly explained that the Spartans did not write down "the laws (*nomoi*) concerning bravery" because young men ought to become accustomed to brave deeds rather than attend to writings. These *nomoi* concerning bravery could not have been an oral set of "laws"; rather, by *nomoi* Zeuxidamus must have meant the customs, traditions, and general moral principles of the Spartans concerning bravery, which together with the whole range of other rules, customs, and traditions (those concerning marriage, social behavior, religious rituals, business contracts, theft, and so forth) formed the undifferentiated totality of Spartan *nomoi*. There is no indication, moreover, that these were ever formalized or recorded; instead they were handed down orally in the form of stories or proverbs of the sort preserved by many ancient authors. We may thus conclude that until the fourth century Sparta had no laws in the strict sense, ex-

18. μὴ χρῆσθαι νόμοις ἐγγράφοις; at what date (if ever) this *rhētra* itself was written down is unknown. See n. 10 above.

19. Boring (1979, 24–31) tends to reject Plutarch's statement that one of Lycurgus's *rhētras* prohibited the use of written laws, but neither of Boring's two examples of early inscribed laws is really a law, as far as we can tell, and the epigraphical evidence seems rather to confirm Plutarch's report; see Cartledge 1978, 35. We might note further that the words Plato attributes to the Spartan Megillus (*Laws* 721E-722A) do not disprove this conclusion. When presented with two versions of a law, one brief and one fuller, Megillus says that the Spartans always prefer the briefer, but if bidden to choose which version he would rather have written down in his city, he would always choose the fuller version. This statement (*pace* Boring) is consistent with the conclusion that the Spartans in fact had no written laws.

20. Plutarch, *Moralia* 221B-C. Zeuxidamus was the son of a fifth-century Spartan king.

cept for the *rhētras*, which may have been written down earlier, though these probably contained only a broad outline of certain constitutional principles. It is reasonable to see the unique situation at Sparta as a conservative protest against the innovation of written laws, but there is no reason to think that by their prohibition of written laws the Spartans were seeking to return to some earlier stage of "oral law."

Let us now turn to the lawgivers, in particular those who were first (or, in Solon's case, second) to write laws for their cities. According to the tradition the earliest of these was Zaleucus.[21] Aristotle[22] tells us that

> when the Locrians asked the oracle how they might find relief from the considerable turmoil they were experiencing, the oracle responded that they should have laws enacted for themselves,[23] whereupon a certain shepherd named Zaleucus ventured to propose to the citizens many excellent laws [*nomoi*]. When they learned of these and asked him where he had found them, he replied that Athena had come to him in a dream. As a result of this he was freed and was appointed lawgiver [*nomothetēs*].

We cannot judge the historical accuracy of the details of this report, but we might note that the general conditions Aristotle describes are similar in several respects to those in other cities that called on special lawgivers at this time.

First, the appointment of a lawgiver often occurs in a time of civic turmoil. In the preceding chapter we noted in Hesiod and in Herodotus's report of Deioces' career how civic turmoil in early

21. I will be dealing throughout with what Adcock (1927, 95) calls the "primary tradition" of evidence about the early lawgivers (see further n. 48 below). For the "mythical" secondary tradition, see the interesting discussion of Szegedy-Maszak 1978.

22. Frag. 548 Rose (= schol. to Pindar *Ol.* 11.17):

ἐπειδὴ γὰρ ἐχρῶντο [sc. οἱ Λοκροί] τῷ θεῷ πῶς ἂν παλλῆς ταραχῆς ἀπαλλαγεῖεν, ἐξέπεσεν αὐτοῖς χρησμός, ἑαυτοῖς νόμους τίθεσθαι, ὅτε καί τις ποιμήν, ὄνομα δ' ἦν Ζάλευκος, πολλοὺς νόμους δυνηθείη τοῖς πολίταις εἰσενεγκεῖν δοκίμους. γνωσθεὶς δὲ καὶ ἐρωτηθεὶς πόθεν εὔροι, ἔφησεν ἐνύπνιον αὐτῷ τὴν Ἀθηνᾶν παρίστασθαι. διὸ αὐτός τε ἠλευθέρωται καὶ νομοθέτης κατέστη.

23. The verb τίθεσθαι implies written laws.

Greece was seen as the result of a breakdown of the legal process, and it is plausible that in attempting to restore stability during such a period of turmoil a city might appoint a lawgiver, either to record some of the community's traditional practices and the established decisions of their judicial authorities or to write new laws on substantive or procedural matters. Other lawgivers who, according to the tradition, were appointed as a result of civic turmoil were Solon[24] and perhaps also Draco[25] in Athens, Pittacus in Mytilene,[26] and Demonax in Cyrene,[27] and others about whom we have no evidence of the reason for their appointment.

Second, it is significant that Zaleucus, whether or not he was actually a slave, was a political outsider.[28] Aristotle elsewhere reports (*Pol.* 1296A18−22) that most lawgivers, including Solon, Lycurgus,[29] and Charondas, were members of the newly emerging "middle" class, which indicates that they were probably newcomers to the aristocratic governments of the seventh and early sixth centuries. The lawgiver (*nomothetēs*) charged with writing a set of laws for a city had a special position in the city that was not part of the normal structure of government. Draco may never have been archon,[30] and though Solon was, he was clearly given extraordinary powers and was viewed as a political outsider. Aristotle says that Pittacus was made *aisymnētēs* in Mytilene,[31] by which he seems to

24. In a substantially preserved poem (4W = 3D) Solon himself describes the turmoil in Athens before his reforms.

25. Many have speculated that the turmoil following the attempt of the Cylonians to take over Athens may have prompted Draco's appointment; see Stroud 1968, 70−74 and cf. Gagarin 1981a, 20−21.

26. References to Pittacus's lawmaking are collected in *RE* 20.2, cols. 1868−69.

27. References to Demonax are collected in *RE* Supplement vol. 3, col. 325.

28. Diodorus Siculus (12.20.1) records that Zaleucus was an aristocrat and was chosen lawgiver after achieving a high reputation in the city, but Diodorus's evidence is thoroughly unreliable, as is indicated by (among other things) his making Zaleucus a pupil of Pythagoras; see n. 48 below.

29. I shall say little here about Lycurgus, the traditional lawgiver of almost all the Spartan "laws," since there is considerable uncertainty about his historical existence, in contrast to the others who, *pace* Beloch (n. 38 below), almost certainly actually lived and wrote laws; see, however, Forrest 1963, 174−79 and Huxley 1962, 41−52, who argue for a historical Lycurgus. The "reforms of Lycurgus," moreover, were probably not written down and thus were not strictly speaking laws.

30. See Stroud 1968, 74−75.

31. See Aristotle, *Pol.* 1285A30-B1, and Newman 1902, vol. 3, ad loc.

mean a benevolent tyrant, though in Homer the word means an
"umpire."[32] And several early lawgivers were foreigners, perhaps
summoned in situations in which discord among the ruling class
was so widespread that no impartial citizen could be found to accomplish the task. Thus Demonax the Mantinean was lawgiver for
Cyrene;[33] Andromadas of Rhegium became the lawgiver for Thra-
cian Chalcis;[34] and Philolaus, a member of the ruling family of Corinth, left that city and wrote laws for Thebes.[35] These examples
show a clear pattern: in a time of civil strife a city would call for a
special person, not currently a member of the ruling class (who
would presumably be too partisan) and in some cases a foreigner, to
write a set of laws for the city.

A third noteworthy item in Aristotle's report is Zaleucus's claim
that he received his laws from Athena. This claim, which was presumably intended to lend authority to the laws, can be compared
with the Cretan view that their laws came from the mythical figures
Minos and Rhadamanthys,[36] and with the Spartan tradition that
Lycurgus's laws came from the Delphic oracle.[37] The claim of divine
or semi-divine origin is not widespread, however, and it certainly
does not support Beloch's argument that all the early lawgivers were
in fact mythical, semi-divine figures to whom various cities attributed their laws.[38] It is quite possible that some, perhaps even many,
lawgivers sought to lend authority to their laws by obtaining oracles
or other stories of divine origin to support and publicize them, but
this does not constitute evidence against the historical existence of

32. *Od.* 8.258. For Pittacus as *aisymnētēs*, see Page 1955, 239; for Aristotle's use
of the term, see Romer 1982. Page (1955, 169–75) argues that Pittacus was a man of
noble rank who only later came to have the support of the common people. Even if
this is true, Pittacus seems to have been appointed to an extraordinary position of
power.

33. See n. 27 above.

34. See Aristotle, *Pol.* 1274B23–26.

35. Ibid., 1274A32-B6.

36. See Plato, *Laws* 624A–625A; cf. the Cretan custom of writing "gods" at the
beginning of their laws, as, e.g., on the Great Code at Gortyn (*IC* 4.72). Pounder's
(1984) explanation that this custom has a Near-Eastern origin is unconvincing; see
p. 128, n. 22, below. For the ascription of the early codes to the gods, see Wolff 1980
(cf. p. 24, n. 16, above) and Pringsheim 1957, 303.

37. Plutarch, *Lyc.* 6.1.

38. Beloch 1912, 350; cf. 1926, 253–58. Beloch's view is now generally rejected,
though Sealey (1976, 104) still suggests that Draco may have really been a snake; cf.
Gagarin 1981a, 1, n. 1.

the lawgivers. Despite certain inconsistencies and contradictions, there is too much evidence concerning the early lawgivers and their laws to doubt their existence, except perhaps in the special case of Lycurgus.[39]

It is impossible to determine from what source Zaleucus derived his laws, if indeed he did have an outside source. One tradition, preserved by Ephorus,[40] reports that Zaleucus compiled his legislation from the *nomima* ("norms" in a broad sense)[41] of Crete, Sparta and the Areopagites, but this observation is presumably based only on parallels later noted and not on historical fact.[42] In fact it is highly unlikely that either Sparta or the Athenian Areopagus had enacted any written laws at this period. The story of an association between Zaleucus and the Cretan Thales (or Thaletas) is reported by Aristotle only to be dismissed as chronologically impossible (*Pol.* 1274A25–31).[43] The tradition of Cretan influence on Zaleucus's laws may have been inspired by the popular view that the Cretans were the first people in the Greek world to have laws, a view perhaps stimulated by the reputation of their mythical kings, Minos and Rhadamanthys, as judges.[44] The tradition that Zaleucus was the earliest lawgiver and was not under outside influence is more firmly established than the tradition of Cretan influence, although it is not impossible that written Cretan laws influenced the Locrians.

39. For Lycurgus see n. 29 above. In a recent article, Van Compernolle (1981) has questioned the historical existence of Zaleucus, arguing that he is more likely to be a creation of the last half of the fourth century. Her arguments, though not persuasive, serve to remind us of the difficulty of establishing any historical facts about this early period. Despite her doubts about Zaleucus, however, Van Compernolle accepts almost all the laws we shall treat as his as belonging to genuine Locrian legislation of the first half of the sixth century.

40. Ephorus *FGH* 70 F 139 (= Strabo 6.1.8, 260D).

41. Ostwald, commenting on Herodotus's discussion (1.65.5) of Spartan *nomima*, says, "this [term] must include laws, customs, usages, practices and beliefs" (1969, 77).

42. See Mühl 1928, 112 for Spartan and Areopagite parallels, and Gilbert 1897, 478 for a Cretan parallel. See also n. 104 below.

43. The case for Cretan influence is argued by Huxley 1962, 43–44 (with 120, nn. 280–82), who is trying to establish the historical existence of Lycurgus, in part by making him a contemporary of Zaleucus. Huxley disregards all evidence to the contrary and finds links between these figures (Zaleucus, Charondas, and Thales) that are tenuous at best. Cf. Szegedy-Maszak 1978, 202–3 on the mythical nature of such attempts to link lawgivers with other thinkers and with each other.

44. E.g., Plato, *Laws* 624A-625A; cf. Aristotle, *Pol.* 1271B20–25.

We shall return to this question in Chapter 6; we might note in passing, however, that there is no evidence for large-scale enactments of laws in the early period in Crete, so that even if the idea of inscribing laws came somehow from Crete, the idea of enacting a set or code of laws probably did not.

Similarly, I am not at all persuaded by Mühl's theory of Near-Eastern influence on Zaleucus's laws,[45] though it may be impossible to disprove it completely. Mühl argues for direct Near-Eastern influence on a variety of Greek laws, including one alleged law of Zaleucus, the *lex talionis*.[46] But even if this was an actual written law and not just a general maxim, it could have developed independently of outside influence.[47] Besides this there appears to be no connection between Zaleucus's laws and those of the Near East, and we thus have no valid grounds for believing the theory that Zaleucus was significantly influenced by Near-Eastern legislation. The enactment of written laws was an intelligent response to a clear need. Scholars, both ancient and modern, are perhaps naturally inclined to attribute an innovation such as this to some sort of external influence, but on the evidence at hand it seems more plausible that the enactment of written laws was a truly original product of Greek archaic culture. We shall also return to this issue in Chapter 6.

Turning now to the laws of these earliest lawgivers, we are not able to determine the exact wording of the laws in most cases, but we can establish their general tenor. Our evidence is fullest for Solon, Zaleucus and Charondas, though some of it, especially in the case of the latter two, is unreliable. In particular, the long account in Diodorus (12.12–21) of the legislation of Charondas and Zaleucus is clearly shot through with later, Pythagorean influence and is thus of little use for our purposes.[48] There is enough other evidence,

45. Mühl 1933.
46. See n. 63 below.
47. Driver and Miles, rejecting the view that Hebrew law borrowed the *lex talionis* from earlier Babylonian law, observe, "Indeed, when once it is realized that the natural remedy for an assault is retaliation, and that talion was a fundamental principle of early law and was only gradually replaced by a system of fixed composition, a similar treatment of similar offences may be expected amongst different peoples in similar stages of civilization" (1952, 408).
48. See Dunbabin 1948, 68–75, who has the best discussion of these two lawgivers; see also Adcock 1927, Van Compernolle 1981, and the brief survey in Graham 1982, 190–91. Mühl (1928) tries to sift out of Diodorus's account those laws genuinely attributable to Zaleucus or Charondas, but his reliance on the alleged

however, that we can still draw a rough picture of the activity of these lawgivers, whose legislation I shall, for the sake of convenience, discuss in four main groups: tort laws, family laws, public laws, and procedural laws.[49]

In the first category—torts—I include any law providing or denying recourse or remedy for a party who suffers damage or injury at the hands of another.[50] Under family law I include most laws relating to property as well as those strictly concerning family affairs, since, at least for the early period in Greece, property was almost always held within and transmitted through the family or *oikos* ("house," "household," "family"), and laws concerning marriage or adoption or inheritance were all primarily concerned with the disposal of the family's property. The third category—public law—applies primarily to the laws of Solon and includes his laws regulating the religious, economic and political life of citizens. Finally, procedural law includes not only laws devoted solely to procedural matters but also procedural regulations attached to or incorporated in substantive laws, such as we find in Draco's homicide legislation. There is, to be sure, some overlap among these four categories, but I think they will afford us a useful structure for consideration of the laws enacted by the earliest lawgivers.

Among the early laws concerning torts we may begin with homicide, which, like most offenses that are considered "crimes" in modern law, was treated in early Greek law in most respects in the same way as today we would treat a tort.[51] We know that as part of his law

---

similarities between certain laws mentioned by Diodorus and other laws known or suspected to be early is methodologically unsound. There may be authentic material in Diodorus's account, but only where it is confirmed by other, more reliable sources are we justified in accepting it.

49. By using these modern terms I do not mean to imply that the Greeks themselves ever divided their laws into such categories; clearly they did not. Nor can we use modern terms with regard to Greek law with the precision of modern (or even Roman) jurists. The legal language of the Greeks was considerably less precise or systematic than that of the Romans or of modern societies.

50. This is slightly broader than the modern category of torts in that it would include damages arising out of breach of contract as well as "crimes" (see n. 51 below).

51. The generalization that ancient law is a law of torts rather than a law of crimes is as old as Maine (1861, 217). The claim is essentially true, for the Greeks at least, though it needs some qualification, especially since it is not easy to distinguish precisely between a crime and a tort even in modern law. Moreover, the various char-

code Draco wrote a homicide law for the Athenians, which remained in force until at least the fourth century B.C.[52] We also have a fragmentary inscription from 409/8 B.C. containing a republication of this law of Draco's,[53] which we shall discuss in more detail in Chapter 4. The law, originally written about 620 B.C., establishes exile as the penalty for homicide and then deals largely with procedural matters: the trial, the obtaining of pardon, and the protection of the killer from the threat of retaliation by self-help. In this connection it is notable that the only other early homicide law for which we have specific information is a procedural law: at Cumae, Aristotle tells us (*Pol.* 1269A1–3), "There is a homicide law (*peri ta phonika nomos*) that if the plaintiff provides a certain number of his own relatives as witnesses to the killing, the defendant is guilty of homicide." We know neither the author nor the date of this procedural regulation, but Aristotle implies that it is an early written law.[54] And though it may be hazardous to generalize from only these two examples, it seems significant nonetheless that in both cases procedural regulations form a very important part of the homicide law. The only other reference to an early homicide law is Aristotle's statement (*Pol.* 1274B23–26) that Androdamas wrote homicide laws which contained nothing peculiar.

Turning now to other torts, one of the reported accomplishments of both Zaleucus and Charondas was to fix precise penalties for certain offenses. Zaleucus did this, we are told,[55] in order that the penalties, which before his legislation had been decided by the judges in each individual case, might be uniform and not vary according to the judge. It is certainly true that in the absence of written laws settlements tend to be determined ad hoc, and even settlements proposed by the same judge for similar circumstances in different cases may have varied considerably. By the mere fact of stating precise penalties in writing, Zaleucus's laws must have changed this, whether or not this was his intent. Charondas too set

---

acteristics distinguishing a crime from a tort, such as public instead of private prosecution and punishment instead of compensation, did not all enter into Greek law at the same time.

52. Draco's homicide law is cited a number of times in the speeches of the fourth-century Attic orators, most notably in Demosthenes 23.

53. *IG* I[3].104 (= I[2].115), excellently republished by Stroud 1968; see also Gagarin 1981a. For a full text of this inscription see chap. 4 below.

54. The contrast between *nomima* ("norms," see n. 41 above) and *nomos* ("written law") seems well established in this passage (*Pol.* 1268B40–69A3).

55. See Ephorus *FGH* 70 F 139.

penalties for various assaults, which apparently were minutely differentiated.[56] Pittacus, we are told,[57] set a larger fine for assault when drunk than when sober; it is implied that the amount of these fines was specified. And the laws of Solon[58] put the fine for rape at 100 drachmas (F 26), and set specific penalties for theft (where the penalty depended in part on the value of the stolen goods),[59] for libel (F 32–33), and perhaps for a dog bite (F 35: the dog must be surrendered wearing a three-cubit-long wooden collar), and even for stealing cow dung (F 64). This last law resulted in a proverbial expression for a petty prosecution.

A number of other early laws should also be included in this category. Among these are Solon's regulations covering the minimum distance from a neighbor's property one could locate a house, a wall, a ditch, a well, a beehive, or certain kinds of trees (F 60–62). We hear of no explicit penalties set forth for violations of these regulations, but they presumably were intended to provide guidelines for settling disputes between neighbors over damages arising from the location of such items too close to another's property.[60] Similarly, we are told that Charondas insisted that goods be paid for and delivered on the spot; any extension of credit would automatically rule out legal recourse since (he felt) anyone who extended credit was himself the cause of any injury he might receive.[61] We might also

56. See the parody in Herondas, *Mimes* 2.46ff. Aristotle remarks on the precision (*akribeia*) of Charondas's laws (*Pol.* 1274B8). Minuteness of detail concerning penalties for offenses was also characteristic of the laws of Diocles of Syracuse, according to Diodorus (13.35), though whether this refers to the fifth-century ruler or some earlier lawgiver is uncertain; see Freeman 1892, 722–27.

57. Aristotle, *Pol.* 1274B19–20; further references are given in *RE* 20.2, col. 1868.

58. I cite the laws of Solon from Ruschenbusch 1966; except where specifically noted I accept his judgment on Solonian authorship, though in many cases we cannot be certain about the matter. Even if Plutarch has his information about Solon's laws at second or third hand, however, and even if laws like that concerning a dog bite, for which we have only his testimony, are perhaps apocryphal, much of his evidence (about the libel law, for instance) is confirmed by other sources. For our purpose it is less important to know precisely what penalties Solon set for various offenses than to know that he did set penalties.

59. F 23; cf. F 24–25. The most complete version of Solon's law on theft is preserved in Demosthenes 24.105.

60. Demosthenes 55, where the plaintiff has alleged that damage was done to his property from a wall on his neighbor's land, may be an example of the kind of situation Solon's law was addressing; see Paoli 1949.

61. Theophrastus, cited by Stobaeus 4.2.20, *ad fin.*: οὗτοι [sc. Charondas and Plato] γὰρ παραχρῆμα κελεύουσι διδόναι καὶ λαμβάνειν, ἐὰν δέ τις πιστεύσῃ,

include here the reports that Zaleucus simplified contracts, and that Pittacus required business to be conducted in the presence of the kings and the prytany.[62] It is quite possible that these regulations had the same purpose as Charondas's, namely to regulate more closely damage suits arising out of commercial transactions. Finally, we should perhaps include in this category the *lex talionis* ("an eye for an eye"), attributed to both Zaleucus and Charondas,[63] though we cannot be sure that this was actually a written law and not simply the expression of a traditional custom or a general principle.

I include one last item related to tort law: the reputed severity of the early lawgivers. The laws of Draco were and still are proverbial for their severity, though in view of the fact that all his legislation except that on homicide was superseded by the laws of Solon, it is unwise to trust the report that he set death as the penalty for all offenses.[64] Zaleucus's laws are also referred to as severe,[65] as are the laws of Diocles,[66] and Pittacus's rule of heavier fines for offenses committed when drunk is also called severe.[67] Whether the verdict of severity would appear justified if we possessed fuller evidence is open to some doubt. Some scholars have assumed that "if we knew

---

μὴ εἶναι δίκην· αὐτὸν γάρ αἴτιον εἶναι τῆς ἀδικίας. Theophrastus is probably referring to Plato, *Laws* 742C.

62. Ephorus *FGH* 70 F 139; Theophrastus, cited by Stobaeus 4.2.20, *ad init.*

63. Our most reliable source, Demosthenes 24.139–41, speaks of the *lex talionis* as an old law (*nomos*) of the Locrians (probably the Epizephyrian Locrians), but does not in this passage mention Zaleucus by name. Demosthenes relates the story that a one-eyed man introduced an amendment to the *lex talionis* requiring anyone who strikes out the eye of a one-eyed man to have both his eyes struck out in return. The story implies that the *lex talionis* was a written law, but the cleverness of the anecdote may cast some doubt on the historical accuracy of its details. Diodorus (12.17.4–5) attributes the *lex talionis* to Charondas, and other later evidence (e.g., Aelian *VH* 13.24) is unreliable.

64. See Gagarin 1981a, 116–21, where I argue that the tradition that Draco set death as the penalty for virtually all crimes is certainly misleading. At most Draco probably set *atimia* ("outlawry") or exile as a penalty in some cases and sanctioned (or refused to prohibit) self-help in others. In either case the offender would be threatened with death if he did not go into exile. All the rather meager evidence for laws of Draco on subjects other than homicide (surveyed by Stroud 1968, 77–82) can be traced to this tradition, almost certainly exaggerated, of his severity. Thus although it is likely that he wrote laws on subjects other than homicide, we cannot trust any of the reports concerning these laws; see also Gagarin 1981b, 73.

65. Zenobius 4.10.

66. Diodorus 13.33; but cf. n. 56 above.

67. Plutarch, *Moralia* 155F.

more of these [early Greek] law-codes we should doubtless be horrified by their crudity and brutality,"[68] but the surviving evidence provides no good grounds for accepting this assumption, and I suspect it reflects a modern (and later Greek) prejudice about "primitive" culture in general. Certainly the surviving fragment of Draco's law presents a reasonable and indeed humane treatment of homicide, and there is nothing brutal or excessively severe in any of the extensive Gortyn laws,[69] many of which must date from the archaic period, or in the other inscriptions discussed below (Chap. 4). Of course certain laws may have prescribed severe penalties, but taken as a whole the judgment of severity is not supported by the surviving evidence.

The second general area of early legislation is family law.[70] Here our information about Solon is considerably greater than about the other lawgivers. We are told that Solon wrote laws allowing men to marry their paternal but not their maternal half-sisters (F 47), regulating the assignment of women to husbands (F 48), prohibiting dowries (F 71),[71] allowing anyone except an adopted son to adopt a son if he has no natural son (F 49, F 58), regulating inheritance (F 50) and "heiresses"[72] (F 51–53), and requiring the support of one's parents (F 53–57). We should probably also include in this category Solon's laws regulating the behavior of women in public (F 72), especially at funerals, where excessive mourning and large expenditures were prohibited, and his law prohibiting a slave from

---

68. Forrest 1966, 144, echoed by Snodgrass 1980, 119.

69. See esp. *IC* 4.41, 4.72.

70. I do not include in this survey the proposed rules of Pheidon of Corinth or Phaleas of Chalcedonia concerning the number and size of estates (see Aristotle, *Pol.* 1265B12–16 and 1274B8–9), since it is not clear that either of these figures wrote actual laws. The report (Aristotle, *Pol.* 1252B14) that Charondas used a word meaning "meal-mate" (ὁμοσιπύους), apparently to refer to a married couple, suggests that he wrote at least one law concerning family affairs, but we have no other evidence as to what that law was. Aristotle's references suggest that family law was a common subject of early legislation, despite the relatively meager literary evidence. The surviving fifth-century laws from Gortyn (e.g., *IC* 4.41, 4.72), many of which were probably first enacted during the archaic period, are largely concerned with family matters; see chap. 4 below.

71. For a recent discussion see Piccirilli 1978.

72. The term *epikleros*, usually translated "heiress," applies only to a woman who in the absence of male heirs is temporarily "attached to the estate (*kleros*)" until some man, normally a relative of hers, marries her and takes control of the property, which will eventually pass to their offspring.

exercising with or forming an erotic attachment to a free boy (F 74). Although it is hard to know the purpose of these last two regulations, it is possible that they, like several of Solon's other family laws, were intended to strengthen the control the head of the family (the *kyrios*) exercised over the other members of the household, and in particular over the women and slaves.

Family laws on similar topics are also reported for Philolaus regulating adoption (intended, according to Aristotle,[73] to preserve a fixed number of estates), for Androdamas concerning heiresses,[74] and for Aristides of Ceos concerning the proper behavior (*eukosmia*) of women,[75] though we are given no details of any of these laws. To the extent that some of Solon's major economic reforms, which we shall examine below, were promulgated in the form of laws, they should perhaps be included in this category, since their purpose was in part the preservation of families and their estates. These include laws that may have been written in connection with the *seisachtheia*, or removal of mortgages,[76] the law prohibiting pledging oneself as surety for a mortgage (F 69), and the law against selling members of one's own family into slavery (F 31a).[77]

As far as we can tell, many if not most of these family laws contained no explicit penalties for violations of their provisions. Private enforcement by the head of the family may also have been envisioned for some of Solon's laws, such as those regulating the behavior of women at funerals.[78] In other cases it is likely that no remedy was stated because the remedy would obviously be a legal suit; in-

73. Aristotle, *Pol.* 1274B2–5.

74. Ibid. 1274B23–26.

75. Heraclides Ponticus, frag. 9.3 (*FHG* II.215).

76. Cf. F 67. This is not the place to discuss the many vexing problems concerning the nature of Solon's economic reforms; for two recent views see Sealey 1976, 107–11, with bibliography p. 128 n. 1, and Andrewes 1982, 377–84.

77. Cf. the law of Locri mentioned by Aristotle, *Pol.* 1266B19–21, prohibiting the sale of property unless a man could demonstrate that a clear misfortune had befallen him, the purpose of which was probably to help preserve the family as well as its property. If Epizephyrian Locri is meant, then the law may well have been one of those enacted by Zaleucus.

78. After his report of Solon's laws regarding the public appearance of women and their behavior at funerals, Plutarch observes that the same regulations exist in his own day (or at least at the time of Plutarch's source; see *FGH* 328 F 65 n. 4): "But in addition our laws provide that those who do such things should be punished by the *gynaikonomoi* ("overseers of women"), since in their grief they wrongly give themselves up to unmanly, womanish emotions" (*Solon* 21.7). This seems to imply that at least with regard to behavior at funerals Solon provided no such penalty, though he may have provided some other form of punishment.

deed such a remedy could be said to be implicit in certain laws. The law governing adoption, for example, stated various regulations concerning the procedure and apparently left it up to anyone who felt deprived of his legitimate share of the inheritance to bring the matter to court.[79] The many inheritance cases surviving among fourth-century orations provide evidence for the operation of such a remedy.[80]

Some of Solon's family laws, however, could not be enforced by means of a private suit (*dikē*), and this was probably why he devised a new procedure for remedying violations, the *graphē* or public suit, which Aristotle calls one of Solon's most democratic reforms.[81] Unlike a *dikē*, which could be brought only by the victim or his relatives, the *graphē* could be brought by anyone who wished. The laws against selling members of one's family or against mortgaging oneself are the only two cases where it is fairly certain that Solon allowed a *graphē*. Violations of either prohibition would leave the victim enslaved and thus unable to bring any suit in court.[82] The procedure of *graphē* may have been instituted by Solon for one other case, that of maltreating one's parents. Such a procedure existed in the fourth century[83] and may have been created in connection with Solon's laws requiring support of one's parents (F 53–57), since an elderly maltreated parent might have difficulty bringing a suit. The new procedure by which anyone who wished could bring a suit in such cases marks an extremely important step in the development of legal procedure and was gradually extended to cover other cases.[84]

79. Cf., e.g., the Great Code at Gortyn (*IC* 4.72), where, although in most of the inheritance laws no explicit penalty is stated for a violation, it is clear that private suits are envisioned in case of disputes, since the laws contain several provisions disallowing a suit in certain specific situations.

80. It is possible that the regular fourth-century procedures for challenging a will were in fact enacted by Solon together with the substantive law, though no evidence survives for written procedural regulations in inheritance cases in Solon's laws.

81. *Ath. Pol.* 9.1; Aristotle does not use the term *graphē* but says that Solon "allowed anyone who wishes to prosecute on behalf of injured parties" (τὸ ἐξεῖναι τῷ βουλομένῳ τιμωρεῖν ὑπὲρ τῶν ἀδικουμένων). In classical Athens such cases were designated *graphai*, though it is possible Solon did not use this term.

82. See Glotz 1904, 369–82, Calhoun 1927, 77–80, and Ruschenbusch 1968, 47–53. A slave did not have the status to bring a suit in an Athenian court, and his master, who would be allowed to prosecute on his behalf, would obviously not want to do so in these cases.

83. On the γραφὴ γονέων κακώσεως see Harrison 1968, 77–78.

84. Calhoun (1927, 80) maintains that "there must have been other offenses

I designate the third general category broadly as public law.[85] In this I include three areas of legislation: religious laws, economic laws, and political laws. This last category includes laws regulating the political activities (in a broad sense) of citizens but not laws regulating the structure of government, for which there is no evidence. Laws covering legal procedure, which could also be included in this category, will be treated separately below. All the laws in this category are from the legislation of Solon.

Among his laws were apparently extensive regulations concerning public festivals and sacrifices (F 81–86).[86] Since we know almost nothing of the situation in Athens before Solon, we must be cautious in going so far as to attribute to him the "foundation" of a religion of the state.[87] Many of his regulations may have simply codified traditional practices, and we do not hear of major innovations of his, on the scale of Pisistratus's reforms of the Panathenaea and the City Dionysia. He seems rather to have elaborated regulations for sacrifices and other religious events. His purpose in doing this is obscure, but the enactment of such detailed regulations may have increased the polis's control of these events.

Several laws of Solon are attested concerning public economic matters, some of which were probably intended to help implement and maintain his economic reforms. We are told of laws requiring people to dig their own wells if they live a certain distance from a public well (F 63), forbidding the export of all agricultural products except olive oil (F 65), restricting the amount of land one could possess (F 66), allowing whatever interest rate the lender wished (F 68), and forbidding any dealing in perfume (F 73), and there may well have been others. Clearly Solon's laws regulated a good many aspects of the commercial life of Athens, and in this he seems to have gone beyond the other lawgivers of his time. The laws of Charondas, Zaleucus, and Pittacus concerning commercial transactions (see above) were apparently concerned only with transactions between individuals and were probably intended to regulate litigation

---

against which Solon undertook to legislate that presented the same difficulties and were dealt with in the same way [sc. by means of a *graphē*]." He may be right, but we have no actual evidence to support this view.

85. The term "public law" is meant to be purely descriptive; the formal division into "public law" and "private law," valid perhaps for Roman and modern law, is not found in Greek law.

86. See also F 77, assuming the ms. reading is correct (see n. 92 below).

87. So Jacoby 1949, 23.

arising out of such transactions and to reduce the amount of such litigation rather than to control the economic affairs of the polis in general. In comparison to these other lawgivers, Solon enacted economic laws of a much wider scope.

Solon's laws regulating the political life of citizens appear to have been equally extensive. He did not write a full-fledged constitution for the city,[88] though he must have made constitutional reforms.[89] We are told, however, that Solon enacted a variety of political laws, among which were laws prohibiting tyranny (F 37),[90] granting the right of citizenship only to certain categories of immigrants (F 75),[91] allowing citizens to form various associations among themselves (F 76), establishing an annual evaluation of every citizen's property for the purpose of determining qualifications for political office and for occasional taxation,[92] regulating the activity of the Naucraries (F 79–80), and regulating public meals in the prytaneum (F 87–89).[93]

The number and variety of these religious, economic and political laws suggest an apparently unprecedented involvement of the state and its legal apparatus in the lives of its citizens and in this respect Solon's achievement was unique. To be sure, we may lack the

88. At least if Solon did write a *politeia*, it was not inscribed on his ἄξονες; see Ruschenbusch 1966, 26, and the works he cites in n. 52.

89. Aristotle, *Pol.* 1273B35–74A22. Some of Solon's constitutional reforms, such as the setting of property requirements for holding office, may have been expressed as economic laws.

90. Even if we are not correct in attributing the law in *Ath. Pol.* 16.10 to Solon (see Gagarin 1981b), *Ath. Pol.* 8.4 indicates that he did enact a procedural law concerning crimes against the state (see n. 111 below). κατάλυσις τοῦ δήμου in 8.4 is undoubtedly an anachronistic expression, but Solon's original law must have included tyranny even if it was more broadly written. The amnesty decree (Plutarch, *Sol.* 19.4) shows that Solon considered tyranny one of the most serious crimes.

91. Exactly what rights were granted to someone who became an Athenian "citizen" (Plutarch's term πολίτης may be only a paraphrase of Solon's expression) is unclear; for some good remarks on the matter, see Manville 1980.

92. *Ath. Pol.* 7.3–4; cf. F 78. The extent of Solon's laws in this area is uncertain; see Rhodes 1981, ad loc. Ruschenbusch 1966, accepting the emendation οὐσιῶν (for ms. θυσιῶν) in Plutarch, *Sol.* 23.3, treats F 77 as part of a law concerning the evaluation of property, but we should probably retain the ms. reading and assign the fragment to Solon's religious legislation.

93. The authenticity of the law prohibiting neutrality in times of internal strife, attributed to Solon in *Ath. Pol.* 8.5 (F 38) is much debated. It is certainly difficult to account for this odd law on the assumption that it is genuine, and I tend to agree with those who see it as a creation of fifth-century propaganda. See most recently David 1984 with references to earlier literature.

evidence for public laws on the part of the other early lawgivers, but given the considerable evidence for their laws in other areas, it seems highly unlikely that they could have enacted a significant body of public legislation of which no trace survives in subsequent literature. It is much more likely that in this one area Solon's legislation was in fact unparalleled. The only achievement we might possibly compare to Solon's is the nearly total regulation of life at Sparta, which, however, was accomplished without written laws.[94] Although I would not wish to press this point too far, it is interesting to note that, as far as we can tell from our admittedly limited evidence, both these cities, which by the fifth century had become the acknowledged leaders of Greece, regulated the affairs of their citizens during the archaic period to a much greater degree than any other Greek city.

Strictly speaking, the fourth general category of early legislation, legal procedure, is a branch of public law, but because of its widespread importance in early Greece it is best treated separately. I have already stressed above (Chap. 1) the importance of procedure in the development of law and have argued against the traditional view of procedural law as "adjective." In that discussion I passed over some of the difficulties involved in making a precise distinction between procedural and substantive law. The two areas are relatively easy to distinguish theoretically:

> Substantive law is concerned with the ends which the administration of justice seeks; procedural law deals with the means and instruments by which those ends are to be attained. The latter regulates the conduct and relations of courts and litigants in respect of the litigation itself; the former determines their conduct and relations in respect of the matters litigated. Procedural law is concerned with affairs inside the courts of justice; substantive law deals with matters in the world outside.[95]

However, although the theoretical difference between those rules that govern the legal institution itself and those that apply to other institutions and are (to use Bohannan's term) "reinstitutionalized" seems relatively unambiguous, in practice matters are not so clear. As Salmond further observes,[96]

94. See n. 19 above.
95. Salmond 1913, 438. See further chap. 1 above.
96. Ibid., 439; Salmond's concise discussion (437–40) of the problem is the most

Although the distinction between substantive law and procedure is sharply drawn in theory, there are many rules of procedure which in their practical operation are wholly or substantially equivalent to rules of substantive law. In such cases
the difference between these two branches of the law is one of
form rather than of substance.

As these remarks suggest, it may be particularly difficult to classify a
law as procedural or substantive when we do not have its exact
wording. Nevertheless, we have considerable information about the
procedural laws of the early lawgivers, which we shall examine beginning with those laws that are most clearly procedural.

Once again our evidence is most plentiful for Solon, though in
this area he does not stand alone. We can begin with Aristotle's famous assessment (*Ath. Pol.* 9.1) of Solon's three "most democratic"
reforms:

First and greatest was the prohibition of debts on the surety of
one's own body, secondly the granting to anyone who wished
the right to seek [legal] redress on behalf of injured parties,
and thirdly (and by this means they say he especially strengthened the people) the appeal [*ephesis*] to the popular law courts.

There is much scholarly disagreement concerning each of these reforms, but it is clear that at least the latter two involved significant
innovations in the operation of legal institutions at Athens. *Ephesis,*
however one interprets it,[97] is clearly a procedure, as is the method
of prosecution by *graphē*, by which anyone who wished could
prosecute on behalf of the injured party, though it is likely that
Solon allowed a *graphē* only in a few specific kinds of cases in which
the injured party would not normally be able to bring suit himself.[98]
I have already mentioned the prohibition of debts on the surety of
one's body among Solon's economic laws. We do not know in what
form Solon expressed his actual legislation on this matter, but it is
certainly possible that he directed that a contract made with one's
person as surety would not provide a valid basis for bringing a legal

---

useful I have seen. Cook 1933 discusses some of the subtle problems involved in distinguishing between substantive and procedural law. See also Bohannan 1965.

97. See most recently MacDowell 1978, 29–33; Rhodes 1981, 160–62.

98. See p. 69 above and also the works cited in n. 82 and Rhodes 1981, 159–60.
Aristotle's language implies that Solon's procedure applied to certain wrongs against
individuals rather than to public crimes, such as tyranny.

suit,[99] and at the same time allowed anyone to prosecute by *graphē* if someone was enslaved for nonfulfillment of such a contract.

In addition to the reforms noted in *Ath. Pol.* 9.1, several other laws of Solon also are clearly procedural. The *dikē exoulēs* (F 36) established a procedure whereby a person who had a clear and demonstrable claim to some property—in particular, someone who was prevented from collecting a settlement awarded him by a court—could sue to collect the amount owed and force the debtor to pay an equal amount as a fine to the public treasury.[100] This law sought to remedy one of the greatest weaknesses in Athenian (and other Greek) law, the difficulty of enforcing a verdict, a weakness still evident in the fourth century.[101] Solon also wrote a law concerning witnesses (F 41) and another law or set of laws (F 42, cf. F 43–44) calling for oaths in the absence of either witnesses or a written contract. From all this it is clear that procedural reforms were an extremely important part of Solon's total legislation.

Procedural regulations also were an important part of the work of other early lawgivers. Aristotle reports (*Pol.* 1274B5–7) that "there is nothing special in the laws of Charondas except for suits concerning false witness, for he was the first to institute the procedure of denunciation (*episkēpsis*)."[102] Another purely procedural law is attributed to Zaleucus, namely a provision that "the party from whom seizure was made should retain possession of the disputed property until the trial."[103] The specific case to which this law applies in Polybius's account concerns the disputed ownership of a slave, precisely the kind of case envisioned by the similar provision at the beginning of the Great Code at Gortyn.[104] Ephorus also tells us that Zaleucus enacted simpler laws concerning contracts,[105] and

99. Cf. the laws of Charondas and Zaleucus concerning commercial transactions (discussed above).

100. Hansen (Isager and Hansen 1975, 144–46) has a good summary of the *dikē exoulēs*; he draws largely on the fundamental study by Rabel 1915.

101. The difficulties encountered by Demosthenes in collecting the settlement awarded him in his first suit against his guardians are recounted in Demosthenes 30 and 31, both delivered in a *dikē exoulēs*.

102. *Episkēpsis* is the formal notification of one's intent to prosecute a witness for false testimony. For the procedure in Athenian law, see Harrison 1971, 192–93.

103. Polybius 12.16.4.

104. For the opening of the Gortyn Code see chap. 4 below. The similarity between this opening and Zaleucus's law may account for Ephorus's statement (*FGH* 70 F 139) that one of the sources of Zaleucus's laws was Crete; see Gilbert 1897, 478.

105. Ephorus *FGH* 70 F 139.

these may have taken the form of procedural regulations. Charondas's law requiring that all sales be made on the spot apparently was expressed as a prohibition against suits arising out of contracts for later payment or delivery, and thus probably took the form of a procedural law.[106] Furthermore, Charondas apparently required citizens to serve on juries and fined the rich heavily and the poor lightly if they did not.[107] Clearly Charondas placed a high value on a properly functioning judicial procedure.

We also noted in our discussion of tort laws the early homicide law from Cumae, mentioned by Aristotle (*Pol.* 1269A1–3), in which "if the plaintiff provides a certain number of his own relatives as witnesses to the killing, the defendant is guilty of homicide." We categorized this as a homicide law, and the early laws at Cumae may well have included substantive laws concerning homicide, but the surviving provision is clearly a procedural regulation. Similarly, as we shall see in the next chapter, most of the surviving text of Draco's homicide law regulates the procedures for conducting a trial, obtaining a pardon, and protecting the accused killer before, during, and after his trial. One of these provisions (lines 30–31) almost certainly referred to the procedure of *apagōgē* or "summary arrest,"[108] which may have been created by Draco. This procedure allowed a person to arrest certain criminals (a convicted killer not in exile, for example) rather than use violence against them (self-help). It can thus be seen, like the *dikē exoulēs* of Solon, as assisting individuals in enforcing the verdicts of the courts.

There were also significant procedural innovations in two of Solon's substantive laws, those concerning theft and tyranny. Concerning theft, as we have seen, Solon set various penalties, which differed depending on whether or not one recovered the stolen goods; he also allowed an additional penalty of five days in stocks to be assessed by the court if it wished. This additional penalty could be proposed by anyone who wished,[109] a new procedure. Thus Solon's law of theft, like Draco's homicide law, apparently combined substantive provisions with innovative procedural regulations.

106. See n. 61 above.
107. Aristotle, *Pol.* 1297A21–24.
108. For a thorough study of *apagōgē*, see Hansen 1976.
109. Demosthenes 24.105 (= F 23d). The additional penalty may have been imposed for thieves convicted more than once, and it is possible that the proposer of the additional penalty may often have been a previous victim. For other views see Lipsius 1905–15, 255 and Hansen 1981–82, 30–31.

Concerning tyranny, as we noted above, Solon may have formally enacted the earlier *thesmion* setting forth the substantive penalty against tyranny,[110] but in addition he probably established a new procedure, *eisangelia* ("impeachment"), in cases of tyranny.[111] Thus Solon's tyranny law may also have combined a substantive law taken from previously established practice with a new procedural regulation. Pisistratus, who became tyrant of Athens despite Solon's laws, reportedly did not change any of these laws but did institute traveling judges,[112] who went around to country villages in Attica to hear cases, perhaps so that the villagers would have easy access to judicial procedure without having to come into the city.[113]

A final group of laws from the early lawgivers must also be classed as procedural; these are the laws intended to guard against any change in the laws. For anyone changing his laws Draco prescribed *atimia* ("outlawry") both for the offender and his family.[114] Solon, who replaced almost all Draco's laws with his own (apparently, we might note, without suffering any penalty himself), imposed a similar penalty on anyone tampering with his new provisions, though he may have exempted the man's family from punishment.[115] And the most famous of these laws is attributed to Zaleucus,[116] that anyone wishing to propose a change in his laws must argue his case with his neck in a noose; if he should lose, he would be hanged on the spot. Even if the details of this story were fabricated, it is possible that Zaleucus took some steps to safeguard his laws against change, since he apparently succeeded, as did Solon and Draco (with his homicide law), in writing laws that endured with very little change for several centuries.[117] The one apparent ex-

110. *Ath. Pol.* 16.10; see Gagarin 1981b.

111. *Ath. Pol.* 8.4 (see n. 90 above). See Rhodes 1979, who rejects Hansen's doubts concerning the validity of Aristotle's report (Hansen 1975, reasserted in Hansen 1980).

112. δικασταὶ κατὰ δήμους (Aristotle, *Ath. Pol.* 16.5).

113. See Andrewes 1982, 407.

114. Demosthenes 23.62. The use of the singular *thesmon* in this provision may indicate that it applies to only one law or group of laws, such as the homicide law.

115. F 93. It is possible that later writers confused Draco's provision against changing his laws with whatever law Solon may have written to the same effect. Dio's report (80.6 = Solon F 93a) that Solon did not penalize the offender's family is not reliable.

116. See Polybius 12.16 and Demosthenes 24.139, which probably refers to Zaleucus (see n. 63 above).

117. See Demosthenes 24.141 (cf. preceding note).

ception to these early attempts to protect one's laws against change was apparently Lycurgus, who, we are told, prohibited the use of written laws in part so that regulations could later be changed as circumstances changed with time.[118] Despite this story, the Spartans were remarkably conservative in preserving their traditional customs even without the help of written laws.

Our survey of the literary evidence for the early lawgivers is concluded. With the exception of Solon, who initiated a large body of public legislation, they seem to have limited their activity to the areas of tort law, family law, and legal procedure, and the evidence indicates that their greatest concern was with the last category, procedure.[119] This is shown by the many laws regulating the judicial system and also from the fact that many laws affecting substantive matters were expressed as procedural laws or were concerned primarily or in large part with procedural matters. It is also apparent that many of the laws led, whether intentionally or not, to expanded use and increased regulation of the judicial process. The recognition of the importance of legal procedure and the evident difficulties confronting it during the archaic period, noted in the preceding chapter, clearly stimulated the same response in many cities: the enactment of written laws regulating several areas of conflict, particularly the area of procedure.

In the area of torts, cities regulated both offenses against people or property (theft, assault, homicide, etc.) and those aspects of social or economic intercourse that often led to conflict (contracts, relations between neighbors, etc.). In other areas too, legislation addressed the evident problems of the community: the gradual breakdown of traditional estates and the traditional family, for example, which seems to have been widespread in the Greek world at this time, and in Athens the economic problems that led to Solon's legislation. In enacting legislation in these areas the early lawgivers were clearly extending the power of the polis over the lives of its inhabitants,[120] a point we shall return to in Chapter 6.

The actual content of the substantive laws they enacted may not

118. Plutarch, *Lyc.* 13.3.

119. Cf. Gernet: "S'il est un secteur où l'on ait chance de voir se constituer une mentalité juridique, c'est celui de la procédure. On ne saurait en exagérer l'importance dans les débuts du droit, et pour l'intelligence même des droits archaïques" (1968, 217).

120. The irony that the family was apparently preserved only through being subjected to increasing regulation by the polis brings to mind the similar irony in Frank-

have been particularly innovative. The penalty for homicide in Draco's law, for instance, was probably the same as it had been in earlier practice,[121] and in other areas the specification and precise differentiation of penalties was probably a greater innovation than the penalties themselves. The many laws regulating previously unregulated behavior may have sought to reestablish rules that had once been taken for granted; Solon's sumptuary laws, for example, or his law against pledging oneself as surety for a debt sound like attempts to eliminate a kind of behavior that earlier had not existed. Even such clear substantive innovations as Solon's law allowing adoptions appear to have been quite restricted in their applications[122] and were probably enacted in response to a pressing need.

Thus the significant innovations of the early lawgivers lay not so much in their creating new penalties for offenses as in other achievements. First, the enactment of written laws in areas previously governed only by traditional customs in itself demonstrated the increasing power of the polis. Second, the setting of fixed penalties for more precisely defined offenses gave the polis greater control over the settlement of disputes in these areas. Henceforth, informal settlements would presumably adhere fairly closely to these official penalties, and the variations among different judges[123] (or among different cases decided by the same judge) would be reduced. Thus even the enactment of a written substantive law setting the traditional penalty for an offense would indicate the greater authority of the polis over people's lives.

By far the largest area of innovation, however, was legal procedure, which the evidence indicates was the area of greatest concern to the early lawgivers. Even where written procedural laws probably incorporated traditional procedures, there was significant innovation in the specification of details. Draco indicates this when after setting forth the precise details of the procedure by which a killer could be reconciled with the victim's family he adds a clause making these provisions retroactive.[124] It was almost certainly possible be-

lin Roosevelt's legislation regulating many of the private institutions of American capitalism in the 1930s.

121. See Gagarin 1981a.

122. Adoption could only take place in the absence of a natural son and an adopted son could not in turn adopt.

123. That there could be considerable variation among the settlements handed down by different judges is implied by Herodotus's story of Deioces (chap. 2 above).

124. For the complete text of Draco's law see chap. 4 below. I have elsewhere ar-

fore Draco's time for killers to be reconciled with their victim's relatives through the payment of compensation,[125] but the process probably involved considerable uncertainty and many killers may have chosen to go into exile rather than risk dealing with the unpredictable relatives. Draco's inclusion in his law of the exact procedural details regulating this reconciliation was thus an important step. Similarly at Cumae, it is likely that witnesses testified in homicide cases before the enactment of the written law specifying the number of witnesses necessary for a conviction, but the specification of a precise number would make the whole procedure significantly different, in that judgments would be more automatic and less subject to negotiation.

In addition to specifying the details of traditional procedures, the lawgivers created several new procedures. Two of these allowed suits to be brought in situations where the traditional procedure was somehow inadequate. The *graphē* was used in cases where the victim or his relatives would normally be unable to bring suit, and *eisangelia* was created for serious offenses against the state where no individual victim may have been able to sue for damages. Two other new procedures were apparently intended to remedy problems in the traditional procedure itself. *Ephesis* apparently allowed litigants in some cases to appeal a magistrate's ruling, and *episkēpsis* allowed someone during a trial to give formal notice of intent to prosecute for perjury at a later time. Other laws regulated various aspects of the legal process, such as serving on juries (Charondas) or collecting one's settlement (the *dikē exoulēs*) or enforcing certain verdicts (*apagōgē*). Clearly the enactment of written laws led to much greater use of the judicial system. Procedure by now was compulsory,[126] and the increasing use of the courts stimulated still more new legislation to remedy defects in the various procedures or to create new procedures. It was a time of turmoil and innovation in Greek law, and much of the creative energy of these lawgivers was directed toward the area of legal procedure.

In sum, the picture we get from these remnants of archaic laws is in full accord with the archaeological and literary evidence. This was a period of increasing economic activity and growing pros-

---

gued that the statement of retroactivity applied specifically to the provisions for pardon (Gagarin 1981a, 52–54).

125. Ibid. 147–50.

126. See chap. 5 below.

perity, marked by frequent periods of crisis and turmoil. The rapid growth in population may have contributed to this turmoil, since the increasing density of settlement would lead to more frequent conflicts between citizens, as is reflected in the various tort laws. The laws also reflect the general weakening of the power and autonomy of the large families and the growth of the idea of the city and citizenship. Although we have good evidence only from Athens, where Solon's laws apparently recognized some kind of citizenship[127] and even Draco appears to associate certain rights with the status of being an Athenian,[128] the very fact of enacting a set of laws for a particular polis would enforce the idea that those who belonged to that polis were specially characterized by an obligation to obey those laws as well as by a claim on the protection offered by them.

The polis was asserting greater control over the lives of its citizens, particularly in the area of legal procedure. Henceforth settlements based on the laws ought, in theory at least, to show less ad hoc variation and less consideration of the status of the litigants. In other words, by the enactment of publicly inscribed codes of law the cities of archaic Greece took a large step toward regulating the lives of their citizens by establishing what we may call the rule of law. The implications of this will be considered in more detail later, but first we must consider the early inscriptional evidence for Greek laws.

127. See n. 91 above.

128. In lines 26–29 of his homicide law, Draco says that if anyone kills an exiled killer who obeys certain restrictions, "he shall be treated just as one who kills an Athenian (τὸν Ἀθηναῖον)." By implication, "an Athenian" is one who enjoys the protection of the laws of Athens.

4

EARLY WRITTEN LAWS:
THE INSCRIPTIONAL EVIDENCE

Our picture of early law-making in Greece, drawn from the literary evidence, is confirmed and amplified by the inscriptional evidence, which also indicates that the Greeks began to write laws in about the middle of the seventh century and that procedural concerns predominate in laws enacted before 500 B.C. There are, of course, difficulties in interpreting the inscriptions, which are usually fragmentary and sometimes of uncertain date,[1] but they have the advantage of being direct evidence and thus not distorted by later interpreters. As a group, moreover, the surviving inscriptions, though not large in number, should represent a more random sample than the literary evidence. Thus the predominance of legal procedure in the surviving early inscriptions may be taken as a more reliable indication of the nature of early Greek law than a similar conclusion drawn from the literary evidence.

The oldest surviving legal inscriptions are probably those from the Cretan city of Dreros, which have been tentatively dated to the middle or second half of the seventh century.[2] One of these is apparently complete:

> The city has thus decided; when a man has been *kosmos*, the same man shall not be *kosmos* again for ten years. If he does

1. For dates I rely for the most part on Jeffery 1961a. She bases her dates, which are often later than those that had previously been assigned, primarily on technical features of the writing, especially letter forms. I shall consider all significant legal inscriptions down to 500 B.C. I shall not be concerned with decrees (Meiggs-Lewis 1969, nos. 5, 14; cf. n. 52 below) or treaties (nos. 10, 17), which are too specific to be treated as laws (see chap. 3 above).

2. Some seventh-century inscriptions recently found at Tiryns may regulate certain cult activities in the city. Regulations pertaining to a single cult do not come under our definition of laws, and in any case these inscriptions are too fragmentary to be of any use for our purpose; see Verdelis et al. 1975.

act as *kosmos*, whatever judgments he gives, he shall owe double, and he shall lose his rights to office, as long as he lives, and whatever he does as *kosmos* shall be nothing. The swearers shall be the *kosmos* [i.e., the body of *kosmoi*] and the *damioi* and the twenty of the city.[3]

This inscription has naturally aroused the interest of epigraphers and historians, who have directed their attention primarily to the evidence the law provides for the political organization of Dreros. The identity of the bodies mentioned in the last clause, especially "the twenty of the city," has been the subject of much dispute.[4] Even a brief consideration of the text, however, shows that the law itself is directly concerned with the legal system at Dreros, and that elements of the city's political organization are mentioned only in passing.

Let us begin with the last sentence of the law. Leaving aside the question of the identity of these political bodies, let us instead ask, what is the purpose or force of this clause? More specifically, what is the nature of the oath to be sworn? Two interpretations of the oath have been given: either the officials swear to observe the law,[5] or they swear an oath in order to "confirm" the law.[6] Neither solution is satisfactory. First, though it is assumed by all that the singular noun *kosmos* is used in a collective sense to designate "the body of *kosmoi*" (cf. Meiggs-Lewis's translation above), and this sense is required by both these interpretations, there is in fact little support for such a use here. Alleged examples of the singular noun in a collective sense are all later than the fifth century and occur only in a few set phrases of ratification.[7] In sixth- and fifth-century inscrip-

---

3. ἆδ' ἔϝαδε | πόλι· | ἐπεί κα κοσμήσει, | δέκα ϝετίον τὸν ἀ-   ←
ϝτὸν | μὴ κόσμεν· | αἰ δὲ κοσμησίε, | ὅ[π]ε δικακσίε, | ἀϝτὸν ὀπῆλεν |
διπλεῖ κἀϝτὸν   →
ἄκρηστον | ἦμεν, | ἆς δόοι, | κὄτι κοσμησίε | μηδὲν ἤμην. vac.   ←
Χ ὀμόται δὲ | κόσμος | κοὶ δάμιοι | κοὶ ἴκατι | οἱ τᾶς πόλ[ιο]ς. vac.   ←

I have taken the translation and parenthetical interpretation from Meiggs-Lewis 1969, 2, but have omitted the letters squeezed in near the beginning of the law, θιοσολοιον, the meaning of which is uncertain (see p. 128, n. 22, below). The inscription was first published by Demargne and van Effenterre in 1937.

4. See Meiggs-Lewis 1969, 3.

5. Demargne and van Effenterre 1937, 346; see also Willetts 1955, 168. Meiggs-Lewis (1969, 3) speak only of "those who swear the oath, presumably every year."

6. Ehrenberg 1943, 17; it is not clear to me just what Ehrenberg means when he says the law was "confirmed."

tions both the singular and the plural occur and (as far as we can tell) the collective sense is never found.[8]

A second objection is that one would expect either that the content of the oath to be sworn should be self-evident, or that some indication of the content should be given in the inscription. But it seems unlikely that it was self-evident that the *kosmos* (or *kosmoi*) should swear to obey the law and the other officials should swear to enforce it. I know of no cases where the officials of a city swear to obey or enforce one particular law, though officials may swear to abide by all the laws of a city,[9] in which case it would of course be unnecessary for them to swear an oath with reference to any individual law. Nor can I find any case where officials swear to confirm or reconfirm a law, a task that here seems especially unnecessary since the law has already been explicitly ratified by the polis (line 1). Thus in neither of the proposed interpretations would the content of the oath be evident, and we must look for some other interpretation of this provision.

The fact that there is no mention of the content of this oath would seem to indicate that the oath should be of a common sort, and the normal context in which oaths are mentioned in Greek laws is that of a trial, where oaths are sworn by judges, litigants or witnesses. The contents of such oaths are not normally specified either in laws or in literary references, since it is easily inferred that a judge should swear to be impartial and judge according to the laws and that a litigant or witness should swear that his plea or testimony is accurate.[10] I suggest, therefore, that the last sentence of this inscrip-

---

7. See the examples given by Oehler 1922, 1495–96, all of which are later than the fifth century, and see also Guarducci's commentary on *IC* 2.v.9.9 (cf. *IC* 3.vi.7.A.2). In later texts the collective singular (if it really is that) generally appears in set phrases, such as κόσμου γνωμά or ἔδοξε τῷ κόσμῳ, and it is not impossible that these reflect a situation where originally a single *kosmos* could decide an issue or enact a law by himself.

8. In the sixth-century inscriptions from Gortyn we find the singular of *kosmos* in *IC* 4.14 and 4.30 and the plural in *IC* 4.29. A recently published Cretan inscription from ca. 500 B.C. (Jeffery and Morpurgo-Davies 1970, see n. 52 below) contains both the singular and plural, and the suggestion that one of these singulars (line B. 3) might be a collective use is doubtful.

9. See, for example, the oath sworn by Athenian officials (described by Aristotle, *Ath. Pol.* 55.5), and perhaps the first clause of the Chian inscription, discussed below.

10. For the judge's oath see inter alia the Great Code at Gortyn (*IC* 4.72) 1.11–12 and passim, and the last clause of the Chian inscription (see below). For a litigant's oath see, for example, *IC* 4.72.9.37–42. See also the first line of the early inscription

tion refers to those who will swear an oath at a trial, presumably a trial arising from an alleged violation of the previously stated regulation. At this trial oaths are to be sworn by the single *kosmos* (presumably the one accused of the violation) and by certain other officials as witnesses (or perhaps even as judges). In other words, these officials are to testify on oath at any trial for the violation of the previously stated law.

This interpretation is consistent with not only the common use of oaths in Greek laws but also the structure of Cretan legal inscriptions, where a punctuation mark (such as the one preceding the last line in this inscription) normally indicates that a separate but related regulation follows.[11] We have other examples at Gortyn of a provision added to the main body of a law giving further information about the procedure to be followed in case of violations,[12] and it seems reasonable to suppose that the additional provision in the Dreros law similarly specifies one aspect of the legal procedure to be followed in case of a violation, a procedure which, as elsewhere in Greece, makes significant use of oaths.[13]

Turning now to the main body of the law, we should note that the only duty of the *kosmos* specifically mentioned is the judging of

from Eretria, discussed below. As we saw in chap. 2, oaths played a part in the preliterate judicial process and the swearing of true oaths is of particular concern to Hesiod in the *Works and Days*.

11. In addition to the mark of punctuation at the beginning of line four, note also that the line begins from the right, though it ought to start from the left to continue the *boustrophedon* order of writing (from right to left and back again) of the first three lines. This is another indication that line 4 is separate from the main text, though whether it was enacted at the same time or later as an amendment is not certain.

12. See, for example, IC 4.72.8.53–9.1, where after a series of laws concerning the marrying of an heiress, a further provision separated from what precedes by punctuation (by means of gap) reads: "If anyone marries an heiress otherwise than as is written, the relatives are to make this known to the *kosmos* [i.e., in court]." See also 6.25ff., 7.40ff., etc. and on the subject of amendments in general, see Gagarin 1982.

13. After working out this interpretation of the final clause of the law, I encountered a similar interpretation proposed by Gallavotti (1977, 130–35) as support for his view that the letters of the first word in line four, ομοται, represent not a noun ("oath-swearers") but the future verb form ὀμοῦται, "he will swear" (i.e., the *kosmos* will swear at his trial). Although I am pleased to find agreement concerning the overall purpose of this provision, I consider a future verb unlikely here, since Greek laws, like most laws elsewhere, are regularly written in the present tense. None of Gallavotti's other linguistically based suggestions affects the points discussed here.

cases. Presumably he had other functions, as we know he did in later times, and these (together with his legal duties) are probably designated by the verb *kosmeō*. But for the makers of this law his most important duty was clearly the judging of cases. This is confirmed by the fact that the first penalty stated for violating the law is that the *kosmos* is to pay double the judgments he rendered. Although the details of this penalty are not specified, it is perhaps more likely that the double payment was made to the city than that it was made to the litigant who had lost a judgment when appearing before this particular *kosmos* during the period of his illegal tenure in office.[14] In either case this would have amounted to a strong deterrent against anyone tempted to assume an illegal term in office, whether in order to hand down a crooked judgment in one particular case or perhaps for some other purpose, such as personal enrichment. Hesiod implies in the *Works and Days* that kings could become rich by means of their deciding cases,[15] and it is possible that some Drerians sought the position of *kosmos* for this reason.

The implication of this sanction and of its prominent position in the law is not only that judicial activity was the most important function of the *kosmos* at this time, but also that the Drerians thought it necessary to enact legislation against at least one possible means of abuse of their legal system. And since laws are rarely passed to prohibit activity that is not already harming or threatening to harm a society, it is likely that this law was prompted by a concern for the proper functioning of the legal process similar to that expressed by Hesiod in the *Works and Days*.[16] We may infer that at least one *kosmos* was thought to have abused this judicial office in the past and that the law was intended to prevent further abuse. A further implication may be that control of the legal system was an important means of gaining power at Dreros. Ehrenberg re-

---

14. See Demargne and van Effenterre 1937, 344. They argue that to have the *kosmos* pay the fine to the losing litigant would sometimes result in an undeserved gain for a litigant who had rightly lost his case. Greek laws often do not indicate explicitly who is to receive a fine (see ibid., 344, n. 4, and the regulations from Eretria and *IC* 4.14, discussed below). For paying a fine to the city in Gortynian laws, see *IC* 4.41.3.17 and the passages cited by Guarducci, ad loc.

15. The kings could profit simply by collecting fees from litigants and not necessarily by accepting bribes in exchange for corrupt judgments; their epithet, δωροφάγοι ("gift-devouring"), is often mistranslated "bribe-devouring" (see Gagarin 1974, 109–10, and cf. p. 30, n. 35, above).

16. See chap. 2 above.

sists this implication, maintaining that "a man who is trying to become a tyrant would hardly do so by way of the judge's bench,"[17] but Herodotus's story (1.96–99) of Deioces' becoming king of the Medes, whatever its historical accuracy, indicates that some Greeks thought otherwise.

In sum, the main purpose of the Drerian law is to prevent the judicial process from being corrupted or otherwise abused for political or financial gain. It is clear from the text that a legal procedure was already formally recognized at Dreros and that a *kosmos* presided at trials and handed down judgments. It is also implied that the use of oaths at trials was already well established. The law prescribes severe penalties for one particular method of abuse of this judicial office and also adds a more specific regulation concerning the procedure to be followed if the law is violated. Thus in both its main text and in the added provision the primary concern of this law is with the proper functioning of the judicial process.

Legal procedure is also a prominent concern in the other legal inscriptions from the seventh and sixth centuries. The six other seventh-century fragments found at Dreros are of little help,[18] but the homicide law of Draco, dating from about 620, is (as we have already noted) largely procedural.[19] The surviving law reads as follows:

17. Ehrenberg 1943, 15.

18. The six other inscriptions from Dreros were published by van Effenterre 1946. Of these (1) is only a tiny fragment. (2) also appears fragmentary and its content is quite uncertain; van Effenterre presents one transcription according to which it is virtually complete, but it is difficult in that case to get a satisfactory sense for the inscription, and it seems better to assume that the writing continued to the left. (3) may have regulated *agelai* ("youth groups") or hunting (see van Effenterre 1961 with a text significantly different from that of his initial publication). (4) has something to do with giving and receiving a share of something. (5) apparently concerns becoming pure (*katharos*) by swearing an oath (for this text see also MacDonald 1956). And (6) may concern religious sacrifices. These fragments suggest that the Drerians may have made laws concerning a wide variety of matters, but with such fragmentary evidence we cannot draw any conclusions about the substance, form, or purpose of these other laws.

19. See chap. 3 above. Draco's law survives (in part) on an inscription of 409–408 B.C. (*IG* I³.104 = I².115), which was republished by Stroud 1968; see also Meiggs-Lewis 1969, no. 86. There has been some doubt as to how accurate a reproduction of the original law this is. The case for a nearly exact copy is strongly argued by Stroud 1968 and is accepted by myself (Gagarin 1981a) and with some reservations by Rhodes 1981, 111–12. Ruschenbusch 1960 (followed generally by Sealey 1983) thinks the surviving text is largely interpolated. The translation is taken, with minor changes, from Gagarin 1981a, xvi–xvii.

Even if a man unintentionally kills another, he is exiled. The kings are to adjudge responsible for the homicide either the killer or the planner; and the *ephetai* are to judge the case. If there is a father or brother or sons, pardon is to be agreed to by all, or the one who opposes is to prevail. But if none of these survives, by those up to the degree of first cousin once removed and first cousin, if all are willing to agree to a pardon; but the one who opposes is to prevail. But if not one of these survives, and if he killed unintentionally and the fifty-one, the *ephetai*, decide that he killed unintentionally, let ten phratry members admit him to the country and let the fifty-one choose these by rank. And let also those who killed previously be bound by this law.

A proclamation is to be made against the killer in the market place by the victim's relatives as far as the degree of cousin's son and cousin. The prosecution is to be shared by the cousins and cousins' sons and by sons-in-law, fathers-in-law, and phratry members. . . . If anyone kills the killer or is responsible for his death, as long as he stays away from the frontier markets, games, and Amphictyonic sacrifices, he shall be liable to the same treatment as the one who kills an Athenian; and the *ephetai* are to judge the case. It is allowed to kill or arrest killers, if they are caught in the territory. . . . If a man defending himself straightway kills someone forcibly and unjustly plundering or seizing him, the killer shall pay no penalty.[20]

20.
10 Πρῶτος Ἄξων
    καὶ ἐὰν μὴ 'κπρονοίας κτείνῃ τίς τινα φεύγειν. δικάζειν δὲ τοὺς
βασιλέας αἴτιον φόνου εἶναι τὸν ἐργασάμενον ἢ βουλεύσαντα. τοὺς
δὲ ἐφέτας διαγνῶναι. αἰδέσασθαι δ' ἐὰν μὲν πατὴρ ᾖ ἢ ἀδελφὸς ἢ
υἱεῖς ἅπαντας, ἢ τὸν κωλύοντα κρατεῖν. ἐὰν δὲ μὴ οὗτοι ὦσι, μέχρ'
15 ἀνεψιότητος καὶ ἀνεψιοῦ, ἐὰν ἅπαντες αἰδέσασθαι ἐθέλωσι, τὸν
κωλύοντα κρατεῖν. ἐὰν δὲ τούτων μηδὲ εἷς ᾖ, κτείνῃ δὲ ἄκων, γνῶσι
δὲ οἱ πεντήκοντα καὶ εἷς οἱ ἐφέται ἄκοντα κτεῖναι, ἐσέσθων δὲ οἱ
φράτορες ἐὰν ἐθέλωσι δέκα. τούτους δὲ οἱ πεντήκοντα καὶ εἷς ἀρι-
στίνδην αἱρείσθων. καὶ οἱ δὲ πρότερον κτείναντες ἐν τῷδε τῷ θεσμῷ
20 ἐνεχέσθων.
    προειπεῖν δὲ τῷ κτείναντι ἐν ἀγορᾷ μέχρ' ἀνεψιότητος καὶ
ἀνεψιοῦ. οὐνδιώκειν δὲ κἀνεψιοὺς καὶ ἀνεψιῶν παῖδας καὶ γαμβροὺς
καὶ πενθεροὺς καὶ φράτορας . . .
26 ἐὰν δέ τις τὸν ἀνδροφόνον κτείνῃ ἢ αἴτιος ᾖ φόνου ἀπεχόμενον
ἀγορᾶς ἐφορίας καὶ ἄθλων καὶ ἱερῶν Ἀμφικτυονικῶν, ὥσπερ τὸν

Although some of the details of this law are disputed, its basic provisions and overall organization are clear. The first section (up to and including the provision for retroactivity) states briefly the penalty for a homicide[21] and the requirement of a trial conducted by the kings and the *ephetai* (officials whose precise identity is uncertain); it then sets forth at some length the rules for obtaining a pardon. I have elsewhere argued[22] that these rules for pardon are probably the major innovation in this first section of the law and were intended to protect both parties in a homicide case from a possibly fatal misunderstanding while they were negotiating a settlement of their dispute (involving the payment of compensation). The epic evidence indicates, as I have said, that before Draco exile was the common result of a homicide. His law officially confirms this penalty, while it also provides elaborate procedural arrangements whereby a killer will first proceed into exile and then, if the victim's relatives are willing, arrange for a pardon (presumably after giving the relatives adequate compensation).

The second part of the law contains further procedural regulations stating that due notice is to be given of a trial and that certain relatives and others will share in the prosecution. Although some of the text is lost in this section, the law probably continued with provisions granting protection to the killer before and during the trial, as long as he conforms to the designated procedure. These are fol-

---

Ἀθηναῖον κτείναντα ἐν τοῖς αὐτοῖς ἐνέχεσθαι. διαγιγνώσκειν δὲ τοὺς ἐφέτας.

30 [ἐξ]εῖ[ναι δὲ τοὺς ἀνδροφόνους ἀποκτείνειν ἢ ἀπάγειν, ἐὰν ἐν] τῇ ἡμεδ[απῇ . . .]

35 διαγιγνώσκειν δέ τοὺς ἐφέτας. [ἐὰν δέ τις . . .] ἢ ἐλεύθερος ἦ, καὶ ἐὰν φέροντα ἢ ἄγοντα βίᾳ ἀδίκως εὐθὺς ἀμυνόμενος κτείνῃ, νηποινεὶ τεθνάναι.

I take the text from Stroud 1968, 5, but have modernized it and have supplemented line 12 *exempli gratia* and lines 30–31, following Stroud.

21. In Gagarin 1981a, I suggest that the first sentence of Draco's law explicitly designates the penalty of exile for unintentional homicide and also, by implication, for intentional homicide. Although I think this is the best explanation of our fragmentary evidence, several other interpretations have been proposed that would not affect the points I make here. Tsantsanoglou (1972), however, has suggested that the first line of the law be restored to read, "even if a man unintentionally kills another, he shall stand trial for murder [καὶ ἐὰν μὴ ἐκ προνοίας κτείνῃ τις, φόνου φεύγειν]," rather than " . . . he shall be exiled." This restoration, if accepted, would make virtually the entire law procedural, but on balance I think it must be rejected (see Gagarin 1981a, 30 n. 1).

22. Gagarin 1981a, esp. 53–54.

lowed by provisions granting protection to the killer in exile and refusing it to killers who are caught in Athenian territory. The final surviving provision is a substantive law describing one situation in which homicide is not punishable.

Judging from this surviving fragment, the main purpose of Draco's law seems to be the detailed elaboration of a procedure for settling disputes arising out of a homicide. The basic settlement (exile) and the basic procedure for submitting such cases to some sort of trial were probably already well established in Athens, but the elaborate procedural details protecting the rights of both parties before, during, and after the trial were probably Draco's innovation. And the fact that this remained the basic homicide law in Athens for at least three centuries testifies to the fairness and intelligence of the provisions.[23]

We must next consider the legal inscription from Chios, dated by Jeffery to 575–550.[24] The inscription (assuming it is all one text) covers four sides of a trachyte stele. Three of the sides are fragmentary and their precise sense is often uncertain, but to the extent that we can decipher it the inscription clearly states important rules of legal procedure. Let me quote Jeffery's summary of the general sense of the law:

> (1) the judicial duties of certain high magistrates are defined, *perhaps* including an oath which reminds them of their duty as guardians of the law of the citizens; (2) penalties are specified, if they (*a*) take bribes or ? (*b*) inflict bodily harm on the person standing trial; (3) in certain circumstances their verdicts may be appealed against; (4) the court hearing appeals is to be the *dēmos, or* a council elected from it which has other

23. Homicide laws are not common in the archaic period, perhaps because homicide was still considered a matter to be settled between the families of the killer and his victim. No mention of homicide occurs in the great inscription of laws at Gortyn (*IC* 4.72). There are, however, a few surviving fragments from Sicily, probably from Leontini, of a law apparently dealing with homicide (*SEG* 4.64). The text apparently refers to certain sums of money, which may be fines. See Jeffery 1961a, 242; she dates the fragments to ca. 525. Pollution from homicide may be the subject of a fragmentary sixth-century inscription from Cleonae (see Jeffery 1961a, 150, no. 6), where Sokolowski's restorations (1969, no. 56) are possible but far from certain. Homicide is also mentioned in one early fragment from Gortyn (*IC* 4.9), and there is a reference to a homicide law in the inscription from Naupactus (discussed below).

24. Jeffery's study of the text (1956) is fundamental. Oliver (1959) supplements many lines to produce a more complete text, but these supplements have not been generally accepted (see Meiggs-Lewis 1969, no. 8).

duties undefined here; (5) the councillors, before hearing appeals, are to swear an oath like that sworn by the judges themselves.[25]

As with the Dreros inscription, much of the modern discussion of this law concerns its constitutional significance, especially the nature and composition of the council (or councils) on Chios and the relation of the Chian to the Athenian constitution. The apparent similarity between the process of appealing a verdict to the popular council and the Athenian procedure of *ephesis*, instituted at about the same time by Solon, has also played a role in discussions of this law. And indeed here even more clearly than at Dreros we can see that the law's basic concern is judicial procedure and its primary objective is to provide safeguards and remedies against possible abuse of the legal system.

In particular, the provision for some sort of appeal to a popular council indicates that the Chians felt dissatisfaction with some of the decisions of their judges. This may have been dissatisfaction with the judicial system in general, or with more specific problems, such as the taking of bribes (perhaps referred to on side A), or the possibility of someone being wronged in the court of the demarch (side B). Evidently the council has other duties too, but the primary concern of this law is clearly its role as a court of appeals.[26] The law further specifies an oath to be sworn, probably in connection with the appeal (side D). Thus by means of an important procedural in-

---

25. Jeffery 1956, 166. Jeffery's translation of the text reads as follows:

(A) '[—] of Istia, guarding the ordinances of the people [—|—]ON:HPEI. If while holding office as demarchos or basileus he ?accepts bribes [—|—] of Istia, let him pay while demarchos; the ?auditor is to exact [the fine, or himself incur it?—|—]EN when the people have been assembled). ??Assaults: a double fine [—|—?a fine] ?in amount the same as that from cases of assault. (B) ?If a suit subject to appeal [—|—], but if he has been wronged in the demarchos' court, [?let him deposit x] stater[s?— and] (C) let him appeal to the council of the people. On the third day after the Hebdomaia let the council be assembled, the people's council, with power to inflict penalties, elected, fifty from each tribe. Let it conduct the other business of the people, and also let it [prepare? or judge?] all those cases which have been appealed against during the month [—|—] (D) of the month Artemision. [—] let him take solemn oath ?and swear [—|—] kings. (1956, 162)

26. The construction τά τ' ἄλλα . . . καὶ δίκας (C.9–11) suggests that the law is not particularly interested in these other matters.

novation the Chian law attempts to remedy certain abuses of the legal system by the magistrates who have traditionally controlled it.[27] Through its function of hearing appeals the popular council clearly gains power at the expense of the (presumably aristocratic) judges. As far as we can tell, however, Chios, unlike Athens, did not sustain this democratic impulse, if that is what it really was.[28]

From about the same period come two very difficult and fragmentary inscriptions. One, from the Argive Heraion (*IG* 4.506) may be a treaty between Argos and other cities[29] or perhaps a list of major crimes against the state.[30] The other, from the precinct of Apollo in Korope in Thessaly (*IG* 9.2.1202) may concern some ritual or may be a prohibition against stealing or misusing the temple utensils for sacrifice.[31] From neither of these inscriptions can we get any clear indication of the content or the intent of the law, if either is truly a law. The Argive inscription may have been a fundamental part of the city's law; the Thessalian regulation probably applied only to the precinct where the inscription stood.

We now turn to the more complete text of an inscription from Eretria (*IG* 12.9.1273–74), dated by Jeffery to about 550–525.[32] A recent study by Vanderpool and Wallace[33] has shown that the inscription consists of four separate texts. The first "stands at the head of a group of more particular laws, and lays down the most general rules for judicial procedure."[34] It reads:

27. Note that these include "kings" (A.4, D.4), whose judicial role may have been similar to that of the "kings" at Athens (see the beginning of Draco's law, cited above).

28. Forrest: "An early start on the road to democracy (marked by the 'Constitution' of ca. 570) does not seem to have led very far" (1960, 180). On democratic tendencies in early Greek laws see chap. 6 below.

29. So Rogers 1901, 173.

30. Jeffery 1961a, 158; she dates the inscription to 575–550.

31. Ibid., 97; she dates this inscription to ca. 550?

32. Ibid., 84. Cairns 1984, 147–48 argues for a date after 525 and reports that Jeffery "would be happy to take the inscription down to c. 525 at least."

33. Vanderpool and Wallace 1964.

34. The translation of this first text is from Vanderpool and Wallace (1964, 389). The Greek reads:

δίκεν ἐπεὰν κατομόσει τίν[υ-]
σθα(ι) τρίτει ἡεμέ[ρ]ει χρέματα
δόκιμα κα[ὶ φ]υγία ἰὰν μὲ τείσε⟨ι⟩

Cairns 1984, 148–53 proposes reading *ἡυ*]*γιᾶ* rather than *φυ*]*γία*; if he is right, a statement of the penalty for nonpayment presumably followed in the next line.

Justice is to be done only after oaths have been administered;
Fines are to be paid on (or before) the third day in good
money; Exile is the penalty for non-payment of fines.

The second text, in a different hand,[35] begins with the name of the
archon but then breaks off, to be resumed in the third text, which
reads:

He is to pay ten staters. If he does not pay, the officials are to
act [sc. to inflict punishment] according to the laws. Whoever
does not so act shall himself owe the fine.[36]

Finally, the fourth text, inscribed later and more carelessly than the
others, may have regulated payments to sailors,[37] but is too fragmentary for any clear sense to emerge.

Despite the gaps, the sense of the two best-preserved texts of this
inscription is clear. The first (and probably the earlier)[38] of these
contains basic procedural rules applying presumably to all trials at
Eretria: the swearing of oaths before a trial, the payment of fines at
a specific time, and the penalty for nonpayment of a fine. The fact
that this law stands at the head of the inscription indicates the importance the Eretrians attached to these basic rules of procedure.
The third text also concerns procedure, in particular the enforcement of settlements. In order that the magistrates might be more
zealous in their enforcement of settlements, the law makes these
officials themselves liable if the assessed fines are not paid.[39] We cannot be certain how general the application of this rule was,[40] but it is
clear nonetheless that the primary concern of this inscription is

35. As Jeffery notes (1961a, 84), the punctuation of the second and third texts is
also different from that of the first.

36.   δέκ[α σ]τατε̑ρας ὀφέλεν
         ἰὰν μὲ τείσει ἀρχὸς ἀπὸ ῥετὸν ποιε̑σα[ι]
         hόστις ἂν μὲ ποιε̑ι αὐτὸν ὀφέλεν

37. The words "sailors" and "pay" are legible in line 1, and two place names
apparently occur in line 2; otherwise "the text remains obscure" (Vanderpool and
Wallace 1964, 391).

38. Ibid., 390.

39. See IC 4.14.g–p.1, discussed below.

40. The provision that the officials should act "according to the laws" may refer
to all Eretrian laws or (less likely) only to those on this inscription.

legal procedure and that these laws are of fundamental importance for the administration of justice in Eretria.[41]

Although the number of these inscriptions is perhaps not large enough to allow us to draw firm conclusions, it is striking that the three best-preserved legal inscriptions from the period 650–525 (from Dreros, Chios, and Eretria) all present fundamental regulations concerning legal procedure, and a fourth inscription (Draco's homicide law), which is probably a nearly verbatim copy of the original law of about 620, also appears primarily concerned with establishing an effective procedure for homicide cases. We have evidence, to be sure, of substantive laws from this period. Some of the early fragments from Gortyn, for example, appear to concern inheritance,[42] and some of the substantive laws on the Great Code at Gortyn presumably date from the archaic period, but in the actual inscriptional remains from the archaic period procedural concerns are dominant.

Indeed, a number of the earliest surviving inscriptions at Gortyn also concern procedure, including the most extensive fragment from this period (*IC* 4.14.*g–p*), which presents some interesting similarities to other early procedural laws. The first line reveals the same rule, that the officials are themselves responsible for uncollected fines,[43] and even some of the same language we found in the third text at Eretria:

> He is to pay fifty cauldrons in each case. If the *kosmos* in charge [of the case] does not exact full payment, he shall owe the penalty himself, and the *titas* [another magistrate], if he does not exact full payment, [shall himself pay?].[44]

The second line of this same inscription states that the same man should not be *kosmos* again for three years. Although this reminds

41. Even if the fourth text does concern payments to sailors, it is not impossible that it too laid down procedural rules for disputes in this area.

42. See, e.g., *IC* 4.17, 20, 21. Jeffery 1961a, 311–13 and 315, no. 2 dates *IC* 4.1–40 to ca. 600–525?. See also the recently discovered fragment from Phaestus (*SEG* 32.908), which may concern property (Di Vita and Cantarella 1982).

43. A similar rule occurs elsewhere in Greece, as Guarducci notes (1950, ad loc.).

44. . . . πεντήκοντα λέβη[τας ϝ]εκάστο καταστᾶσαι. ϙόσμος ὁ ἐπιστάς : αἰ μὴ ἐστείσαιτο, ἀϝτ[ὸν ὀ]πήλεν : καὶ τὸν τίταν : αἰ μὴ 'στείσαιτο τ[. . . ; cf. n. 36 above.

us of the early law from Dreros (discussed above), we do not in this case have any indication of the law's purpose; it is clear from the first line that the *kosmos* had legal duties, but it is not clear whether the restriction of his term to three-year intervals has anything to do with his role in the legal process. This Gortynian inscription reinforces our conclusion, however, that, even allowing for the possibility that the inscriptional evidence is not fully representative, procedural laws must have formed a large and important part of early Greek legislation.[45]

Only one other text remains to be considered, a late sixth-century bronze plaque with regulations concerning the inheritance and inalienability of rural allotments, probably from the Locrian colony of Naupactus.[46] The text gives rules for the inheritance of a family's portion of pasture land under various conditions and sets forth penalties for the violation of these rules, except in an emergency. The rules appear to apply to a new territory being divided up, though the reference to a homicide law apparently already in existence (lines 13–14)[47] may suggest that the promulgators of the law "are an old community extending their interests into a new area."[48] As we saw in the preceding chapter, laws concerning family property and inheritance were common in Greece at this time and they might be especially needed in new colonies or new divisions of land, as they are here. Provisions similar to these were undoubtedly in effect elsewhere.[49]

We should note that the expression designating a homicide law (*andrephonikos tetthmos* [= *thesmos*]) almost certainly refers to a written law.[50] In contrast to this, in lines 5–6, at the end of the list of heirs specifically mentioned (son, daughter, brother), the law states that the right of pasturage (if this is the meaning of *epinomia*) shall

45. I skip over many other early fragments of Cretan laws, since even where these appear to be procedural (e.g., *IC* 1.8.2) or substantive (e.g., *IC* 2.5.1), we can get no clear idea of the content, form, or purpose of the law.

46. Meiggs-Lewis 1969, no. 13. Jeffery 1961a, 104–5 dates the plaque to ca. 525–500.

47. Although there is considerable uncertainty about the precise sense, lines 9–14 apparently prescribe that anyone who violates the rules for the distribution of land shall be accursed, his property confiscated, and his home demolished "just as in the homicide law" (κὰτ τὸν ἀνδρεφονικὸν τετθμόν).

48. Meiggs-Lewis 1969, 25; cf. Jeffery 1961a, 105–6.

49. See Asheri 1963, esp. 1–4.

50. Cf. the use of τεθμὸς ὅδε in line 1 to refer to the law on this inscription.

in the absence of brothers pass to the other relatives according to *to dikaion*, that is, "according to what is right or just" and not "according to the law," as Meiggs-Lewis translate.[51] We should hardly expect that these inheritance rights were spelled out in much greater detail in a separate law, but it is perfectly plausible that an inheritance law should specify the order of the first three relatives in line of succession and then leave the remaining line of succession (if the occasion should ever arise) to be determined "according to what is right." This inscription thus indicates that the Greeks themselves at this time made a clear distinction between a *thesmos*, or written law, and *to dikaion*, an unwritten general sense of what is right.

The above survey of the surviving inscriptional evidence for Greek laws before 500 B.C.[52] has confirmed the conclusions we reached in the preceding chapter. The subjects treated by the early lawgivers according to the literary tradition, namely torts, family law, and especially legal procedure, are also treated in the surviving inscriptions. The inscriptions suggest even more strongly, however, that the early Greeks placed great emphasis on procedural rules.

Given the preponderance of procedural law in the inscriptions, there is little we can add to the conclusions drawn at the end of the last chapter with regard to substantive law. We have already noted that Draco probably kept the traditional penalty for homicide. The early fragmentary inscriptions from Gortyn (*IC* 4.1–40)[53] contain numerous references to amounts of money, expressed in terms of tripods or cauldrons, which probably designated fines for specific offenses. We may suppose that during this period the Gortynians set precise penalties for a large number of offenses,[54] and if this is an

51. Meiggs-Lewis 1969, 24.

52. I have not discussed two recently published Cretan inscriptions. One, in the British Museum, is dated around 500 B.C. (Jeffery and Morpurgo-Davies 1970). It is apparently a decree (cf. n. 1 above) concerning one man, Spensithios, who is being appointed scribe for the city. Beattie's suggestion (1975, 26–30) that ποινικάζεν in this inscription is derived from ποινή and thus refers to the judging of homicide or similar cases is adequately refuted by Edwards and Edwards 1977. The other inscription, from Lyttos, contains two difficult texts from perhaps the first quarter of the fifth century (van Effenterre and van Effenterre 1985). The first regulates the treatment of foreigners in the city, the second the public gathering of domestic animals.

53. For the date of *IC* 4.1–40 see n. 42 above.

54. Cf. the possible mention of fines in the fragments from Leontini (n. 23 above). We cannot tell whether these were fines for homicide itself or for violations of other rules concerning the settlement of homicide cases.

accurate conclusion, it supports the literary evidence that the early lawgivers set precise, finely differentiated penalties for offenses.

The procedural laws on inscriptions show several common tendencies. There is considerable concern with the behavior of magistrates, as seen in laws limiting their term in office, allowing appeals from their decisions, and requiring them to enforce settlements. This last matter seems to have been of concern throughout Greece. It appears that when judicial procedure became compulsory,[55] litigants who won their cases still had no means of enforcing judicial settlements other than self-help. Solon's *dikē exoulēs*[56] was one response to this problem; a similar response is seen in the first section of the Great Code at Gortyn (*IC* 4.72). Although this code was inscribed around 450, it probably contains considerable material that had earlier been inscribed elsewhere,[57] and so may be used to shed light on the legislation of archaic Gortyn.

The first section of the Code (1.2–2.2) prohibits the seizure of a free man or of someone else's slave; violators must release the seized person before the trial.[58] Much of this section after the opening statement of this rule concerns the possibility that a litigant will not release the person either before the trial or after having received an adverse judgment, and various fines are provided in this event, including a tripling of fines after one year.[59]

These provisions confirm the conclusion that the enactment of laws setting explicit penalties and procedures did not automatically insure the enforcement of these laws. At first enforcement must have been entirely in the hands of the winning litigant, but gradually the polis tried to assist him in various ways. In some cases a law was enacted providing stiffer penalties for nonpayment of legal settle-

55. See chap. 5 below.

56. See chap. 3 above.

57. See Gagarin 1982, 138–40, where I argue that the first section of laws (1.2–2.2) was composed in several stages, the earliest of which was the enactment of 1.2–12. See Willetts 1967 for a translation and commentary on this famous inscription.

58. This traditional interpretation of the law has recently been challenged by Rosén (followed by van Effenterre 1983), who argues that the first sentence of the law means "whoever is going to contend (in court) *against* a slave or a free man is not to seize [the object of dispute] before a trial" (1982, 11). I find this interpretation utterly unconvincing (and it is now refuted by Maffi 1983, esp. 3–22). Even if Rosén is right, it would not substantially affect my argument.

59. See Gagarin 1982, 139, n. 38.

ments, sometimes in the form of fines payable to the public treasury instead of or in addition to the victim (as in the *dikē exoulēs*); in other cases (Gortyn) a law declared the magistrates who handed down decisions responsible for their enforcement. Both methods are used in the law from Eretria. Presumably these laws were at least partially effective, though we know that even in fourth-century Athens the enforcement of decisions was often a difficult matter.

Throughout the early inscriptions there is an evident trend (noted already in the literary evidence) to restrict or regulate the power of the magistrates involved in the judicial process. We should also note that the use of oaths in legal procedure is quite common on the inscriptions. The laws provide little information about the content of these oaths, probably because the content is self-evident: that is, judges swear to be fair and follow the laws, and litigants and witnesses swear to present their cases and testimony accurately.

Finally, it is interesting that the inscriptions give no evidence of large-scale enactments of laws during the archaic period such as we read of in the literary evidence. This does not necessarily mean the literary evidence is wrong, since the earliest sets of laws may well have been inscribed on perishable materials, as we know were the laws of Draco and Solon.[60] In Crete, however, we have clear evidence that the earliest laws were single enactments and were inscribed separately.[61] We shall examine this situation more fully in Chapter 6.

Having assembled the evidence for law in archaic Greece, we shall in the next two chapters consider more general issues, first (in Chapter 5) the nature of justice during this period and the ways in which it may have changed or developed, and then (in Chapter 6) the reasons why the Greeks first wrote down laws.

60. See p. 127, n. 18, below. The recently discovered sixth-century inscription from Phaestus (see n. 42 above) may have been part of a larger inscription, in which case this would be the earliest evidence for large-scale inscription of laws in Crete.

61. See p. 138, n. 52, below.

5

JUSTICE IN EARLY GREECE

In the three preceding chapters we have assembled the evidence for
legal procedure and substantive, written law in early Greece, on the
basis of which we may now examine some of the general features of
early Greek justice. Throughout this discussion I shall be using
"justice" in a relatively restricted sense to designate the legal process by which disputes are settled and the substantive norms which
help determine the content of these settlements. I exclude, in other
words, matters of "morality" and religion, except as these may enter
into legal contexts. Thus, the only aspect of "the justice of Zeus," as
it is often called, that shall concern us is the god's interest in judicial
procedure. Zeus gave "law" (*dikē*) to men, Hesiod says (*WD* 279),
and both Homer and Hesiod attribute to Zeus a general oversight of
human justice.[1] Clearly Zeus's concern is consistent with and supports the high value the early Greeks (as we saw in Chapter 1) put
on legal procedure. But Zeus seldom involves himself directly in the
settlement of human disputes, and it may be that the rules or principles governing human behavior toward the gods (and the punishment of violations of these rules) differ significantly from those rules
governing behavior among mortals that are subject to judicial procedure. My own concern here is only with this latter area.[2]

With regard to human justice I am in substantial agreement with
Havelock's view that justice in early Greece was "a procedure not a
principle" and that no Greek at that time would have thought to ask
the question 'What is justice?'[3] Nonetheless, we may still seek to
discover certain general rules or principles underlying early Greek
justice. Even if the Greeks themselves could not, or at least did not,

---

1. E.g., *WD* 9, 248–73, *Iliad* 16.387–88; see Gagarin 1973, 91–92.
2. Questions concerning the nature of early Greek morality or the "justice" of
the Greek gods are complex, and any discussion should begin with a clear definition
of the basic concepts of morality and justice. I plan to treat these questions in a future work.
3. Havelock 1978, 137 and passim.

form explicit generalizations, we may still ask what were the general characteristics of, on the one hand, a just (or fair, or straight[4]) procedure for settling disputes and, on the other hand, of a just (or fair, or straight) settlement.

The early Greeks probably did not distinguish sharply between a just procedure and a just final settlement. The word *dikē* can designate either the procedure, or the settlement, or both.[5] In the system for settling disputes that prevailed in early Greece, in which disputes were voluntarily submitted for settlement, a just settlement (that is, a settlement acceptable to both sides) would be the normal result of a just procedure. Nonetheless, we can still make the distinction between procedure and settlement, and for the purpose of our own analysis it is best to keep the two separate. Let us begin with settlements: what criteria might guide a litigant or others in the community in assessing the justness or straightness of a proposed settlement?

Two general considerations seem to apply. First, the settlement should be consistent with the society's generally accepted norms of behavior,[6] and second, there should be compensation in the form of restitution or retribution (or both) for any damages suffered, whether for physical damage to a person or his property or for less tangible damage inflicted on a person's honor or *aretē*.[7] The first of these principles stems from the tendency, observable everywhere in human society, for the habitual behavior of a community to become normative, that is, prescriptive as well as descriptive. The second stems from the fact that at least one party to a dispute usually sees himself as injured and feels the need for compensation, which any settlement acceptable to him must provide, or appear to provide.

---

4. On the connection between "just" (*dikaios*) and "straight" (*ithys*), which may be explicable on the theory that *dikē* ("justice") originally designated a boundary mark, see Palmer 1950 and p. 48, n. 83, above.

5. *Dikē* and its derivatives have a broad set of applications and can refer either to the legal process and its proper functioning or to social norms and proper behavior; see Gagarin 1973 and the discussion of Hesiod's *Works and Days* in chap. 2 above.

6. I do not mean to imply that these norms are explicitly expressed in Homer or anywhere else in early Greece; as Havelock has shown (1978, esp. 106–22), the Homeric poems usually present norms only implicitly by means of both positive and negative example. A variety of norms are explicitly stated in Hesiod's *Works and Days*.

7. Cf. Hesiod, *Theogony* 89, where wise kings are said to "accomplish restitution" (μετάτροπα ἔργα τελεῦσι).

Both of these general rules contain, however, certain ambiguities, and there is consequently a considerable variation in the application of either rule to a specific case. First, since the norms of preliterate Greece are neither written down nor in most cases explicitly formulated, they are not precise enough or internally consistent enough to provide a clear guide for behavior. Second, there is considerable ambiguity in the demand for compensation, which may sometimes be satisfied by simple restitution or even by soothing words, but at other times seems to require a virtually unlimited degree of retribution. Thus there is often a considerable difference of opinion as to what constitutes adequate compensation in a particular case, and the presence of emotional factors and considerations of social status only increase the apparent arbitrariness of the demand. The effect of this ambiguity is most easily seen if we examine the norms governing settlements and the demands for compensation in several actual cases.

We may begin with the chariot race in Book 23 of the *Iliad*, where the basic rule is relatively clear: prizes are to be awarded to the contestants in the order of finish. In this case ambiguity results from a discrepancy in two cases between the natural swiftness of each charioteer's horses, which is apparently set from the beginning,[8] and the actual order of finish. In the first case the contestant who ought to be the fastest of all, Eumelus, has an "accident" (prompted by Athena) and comes in last. Achilles, however, observing that "the best man [*aristos*] has come in last," decides to give Eumelus the prize for second place (23.536–38); Diomedes, who came in first, wins the first prize. All the Achaeans approve this plan except Antilochus, who claims the second-place prize himself on the ground that he was the actual second-place finisher. He suggests that Achilles give Eumelus a special prize, which Achilles agrees to do, thereby preventing the outbreak of this potential dispute.

From this it appears that two different courses of action may be proper for Achilles and acceptable to the other Achaeans in general: to award the prize to the actual second-place finisher (Antilochus) or to give it to the one who ought to have finished first but actually came in last. The conflict between these two standards may poten-

8. The order in which the contestants come forth to compete (23.287–351) corresponds exactly to the speed of their horses: Eumelus, Diomedes, Menelaus, Antilochus, Meriones. For the details of the race see Gagarin 1983 and the discussion in chap. 2 above.

tially lead to a serious dispute, since Antilochus threatens to fight for the prize if necessary, but a compromise solution is reached, acknowledging the claims of both men and acceptable to both (and also to Achilles and presumably the rest of the crowd). The final settlement in this case thus provides no guidance in eliminating this conflict between norms; instead it ambiguously reaffirms both of the conflicting norms that initially produced the dispute.

The dispute between Menelaus and Antilochus, though more complex, involves a similar ambiguity in the awarding of the prize for second place once Eumelus is no longer under consideration: should it go to the actual second-place finisher (Antilochus) or to Menelaus, who ought to have finished ahead of him according to the inherent speed of his horses? This question then leads to another: when Antilochus overtook Menelaus by means of his boldness and skillful driving, did he employ a legitimate tactic? The claims of both men appear to be valid, and in this case too a compromise settlement is reached in which each can consider the prize rightly his own, though in the end Antilochus actually receives the mare, while Menelaus obtains instead a satisfactory acknowledgment of his greater *aretē* (together with the third prize). Thus Menelaus receives what he considers to be adequate compensation for his loss (as he sees it) of the second prize, and Antilochus keeps the prize, which he regards as rightly his. The question whether Antilochus's overtaking of Menelaus was a legitimate tactic or a violation of normal or proper racing behavior is left without a clear answer, since both his skillful ploy and Menelaus's more traditional sense of *aretē* are apparently validated by the final settlement. And the same conflicting norms as in the preceding case are once more both ambiguously reaffirmed, since each man in the end sticks to his claim that the second-place prize is rightfully his,[9] while at the same time generously offering it as a gift to the other.

The quarrel between Agamemnon and Achilles also concerns conflicting norms and disputed compensation. In this case there is, however, one clear norm: Agamemnon's initial refusal to let the priest, Chryses, ransom his daughter, which is the ultimate cause of the quarrel, clearly violates the rules for treatment of a priest and is viewed as improper by everyone, including Agamemnon himself in the end. When he is then forced by the plague and the prophet's

9. Antilochus in 23.592; Menelaus in 23.610.

interpretation of it to let Chryses have his daughter without any ransom, Agamemnon asserts his right to take a slave-girl from any of the Achaeans and eventually takes Briseis from Achilles. This act is clearly foolish; [10] it results from a fit of anger and causes an unnecessary diminution of honor for Achilles, the leading Greek fighter. But not even Achilles himself questions Agamemnon's right, as leader of the expedition, to take Briseis for himself, and Achilles would clearly not be justified in attacking Agamemnon physically, as he initially thinks of doing. On the other hand, Achilles is clearly within his rights in retiring from the fighting, though his act of anger and defiance causes unnecessary loss of life among the other Achaeans. They can only plead with him to return; he is under no explicit obligation to do so (though we might consider him under a "moral" obligation). To the extent that both men are acting selfishly and in anger, their behavior is open to criticism and is in fact criticized explicitly and implicitly by Nestor when he proposes a settlement (*Iliad* 1.274–84), but both men are acting within their acknowledged rights and neither violates a specific norm.

The conflicting norms underlying this quarrel are more general than those in the chariot race and have several different aspects. Perhaps most basic is the conflict between two individual applications of the same basic norm, namely that personal honor and glory should be achieved at almost any cost. According to the competitive standards of Homeric society,[11] both Agamemnon and Achilles are at least to some extent justified in seeking their own glory and honor at the expense of others. In general, however, it is clear that this extremely important norm of behavior is inherently conducive to conflict in the society.

Another aspect of the dispute is the conflict each man faces between this striving for honor and the need to consider the welfare of his fellow soldiers, who may be competing for the same glory, which is essential to the success of a military venture. In the end Achilles, because of his greater strength and his extreme stubbornness, manages both to achieve his own personal glory and to contribute to the army's success in battle, despite much loss of life, whereas Agamemnon gains no glory and only barely manages to achieve success as commander of the army.

10. See Agamemnon's famous declaration (*Il.* 19.85ff.) that he was the victim of *atē* ("delusion").

11. These competitive standards are well analyzed by Adkins 1960 and 1982.

Once it becomes clear that Achilles has the upper hand because he is indispensible to the military success of the expedition, the dispute then centers on the question of adequate compensation for his loss. Agamemnon is willing to offer material gifts of almost any value, while Achilles first refuses (in Book 9) to accept any compensation and then, after he has decided to reenter the battle, declares the compensation irrelevant (19.146–48). It is clear that his estimate of adequate compensation for his loss depends almost entirely on emotional factors and is heavily conditioned by his sense of his own special status in the Greek army.

The poem conveys a fairly clear sense, however, that it is unreasonable and improper for Achilles to refuse any compensation at all, and his rejection of the embassy in Book 9 meets with virtually unanimous disapproval. This episode, and indeed the whole poem, implicitly confirms the general rule that one should accept a reasonable amount of compensation for a loss, give up one's anger after a time, and settle one's disputes peacefully.[12] At the same time, however, by reaffirming the conflicting norms underlying the dispute the poem gives no guidance at all for the resolution of similar disputes, and, as far as the poem is concerned, the competitive norms it fosters will likely continue to produce similar conflicts in the future.

In contrast, the dispute between Odysseus and the suitors seems to validate the rejection of a peaceful settlement in favor of the use of self-help to obtain one's desired compensation.[13] The dispute itself stems from the conflicting set of rules guiding the behavior of both the suitors and Penelope in the ambiguous situation of Odysseus's extremely long absence. As legitimate suitors of a woman who has indicated that she will soon decide to select one of them to be her new husband, they have a right to be entertained in Odysseus' house until she makes this decision. In several respects, however, their behavior in the house is clearly improper; moreover, most of them obviously violate the norms for proper treatment of a beggar, and their plan to kill Telemachus is a clear violation of several norms.

We, of course, know from the beginning of the poem that Odys-

12. Cf. Ajax's admonition (*Il.* 9.632–36, discussed in chap. 1 above) that even after the killing of a close relative, a man gives up his anger and is reconciled with the killer.

13. For this reason Havelock may be right to argue (1978, 148–49) that paradoxically the *Iliad* shows a more advanced sense of "justice" than the *Odyssey*.

seus is alive, and since the story is for the most part told from his point of view,[14] the reader tends to sympathize with his position in the dispute and to agree with his rejection of the suitors' offer of compensation that they make once he clearly has the upper hand in the conflict.[15] For Odysseus and his patron Athena only the death of all the suitors will be adequate compensation for what he has suffered, and his position seems to be validated by the events at the end of the poem, particularly by the continued intervention of Athena.[16] His primary motivation seems to be not the material damages inflicted on his household but the psychological threat to his wife's virtue and his own honor, and it may be Eurymachus's failure to understand this emotional factor that leads him to make his offer of compensation in purely material terms. The final outcome does not, however, provide any clear guidance for behavior in such ambiguous situations. The lesson, if any, seems to be that one should end up on the winning side, and the conflict of norms inherent in the suitors' ambiguous situation remains unsolved.

The picture that emerges from these Homeric cases could be amplified by the other cases discussed in Chapter 2, particularly the dispute between Hermes and Apollo: the theft of the cattle is clearly wrong in some sense and requires compensation, and yet Hermes quite openly profits from it and in the end achieves the honor he was seeking. Thus the poem as a whole seems to validate his behavior. It is sufficiently clear by now, however, that disputes in early Greece tend to arise out of conflicting or ambiguous norms; seldom are the facts in dispute. When these disputes are settled, certain norms appear to be reaffirmed, but the conflict or ambiguity is not resolved and the settlements provide no clear guidance for the settlement of similar disputes in the future. This is in part because the settlements sometimes appear to reaffirm conflicting norms (as in the dispute

14. See, however, *Odyssey* 24.120–90, where the suitors' complaints are voiced; and see Havelock 1978, 143–44 for a good discussion of the "dubiety of issues" in the *Odyssey*.

15. *Odyssey* 22.54–59; see chap. 2 above.

16. Athena sees to it that all the suitors are present for Odysseus's final slaughter, as we learn first when, the poet tells us, she urged Odysseus to gather bits of bread from the suitors "and so learn which of them are decent (*enaisimoi*) and which are lawless (*athemistoi*), but even so she was not going to save any of them from ruin" (17.363–64). This information is confirmed later when Odysseus urges one of the decent suitors, Amphinomus, to leave so that he will be spared, but "Athena set fetters on him to be slain by the spear and hands of Telemachus" (18.155–56).

between Antilochus and Menelaus), and also because almost all the settlements seem largely conditioned by qualities specific to the people involved in the dispute. The relative power of the disputants, which includes not just their physical strength but also their status or *aretē*,[17] their rhetorical ability, and various other factors, is a crucial element influencing the terms of the final settlement. In addition, emotional factors play a large role in many settlements.

In short, settlements in preliterate (proto-legal) Greece, as in other preliterate societies, tend to be ad hoc, determined as much by the particular natures of the two disputants as by the objective nature of the "crime" or the situation in general. Settlements often reaffirm certain general rules of behavior, but they rarely give any specific guidance for future settlements,[18] such as might come from more authoritative judgments in a system of compulsory litigation or from clearer, more specific, and more authoritative rules, that is, from written laws. Despite the various ambiguities in the settlement of disputes in Homer, however, two very general principles seem to be universally upheld, however loose and unpredictable their application in a specific case: the adherence to, or restoration of, norms of proper behavior, and compensation for damages, whether by restitution, or retribution, or both.

We can be briefer about the general characteristics of a just procedure in preliterate Greece, since we have already examined most of the evidence in Chapter 2. Despite the implicit message of Odysseus's victory over the suitors (that extralegal means of retaliation are commendable), it is clear from the *Iliad* and the *Works and Days*, as well as the later works we examined, that the Greeks placed a high value on an effective procedure for settling disputes peacefully. Odysseus's description of the Cyclopes as having neither councils (*agorai*) nor traditional judgments (*themistes*) but living apart in caves, dealing out justice to their own families and paying no heed to one another (*Odyssey* 9.112–15) implies that as early as Homeric times, the Greeks saw the settlement of disputes as characteristic of a civilized society.[19] The same implication is apparent, as we have noted, in the trial scene on Achilles' shield.

17. Cf. Maine's often-cited observation that "the movement of the progressive societies has hitherto been a movement *from Status to Contract*" (Maine 1861, 100).

18. Cf. Comaroff and Roberts 1981, 236–38, where they discuss the unpredictability of many types of dispute settlement among the Tswana.

19. Cf. also Odysseus's description of the Cyclops, Polyphemus, as "wild, knowing neither settlements (*dikai*) nor traditional judgments (*themistes*)" (9.215).

The characteristics of an effective procedure are clear and consistent: both parties should submit their dispute voluntarily (though perhaps at the urging of others) for a public settlement, both litigants should be able to speak their case,[20] and a settlement should be reached that is acceptable to both. Such a procedure is designated as "straight," which in reference to the whole procedure or the final settlement seems to mean "fair"—a straight settlement evenly divides the opposing claims—and in reference to the pleas of the litigants seems to mean "truthful." Thus to speak a straight *dikē* involves both telling the truth, which may be guaranteed in some cases by the swearing of an oath, and proposing a settlement that will be acceptable to both parties, which may require the rhetorical ability to persuade them to accept it. In a properly functioning system the two litigants and the judge will all speak straight *dikai*, and the result will be a straight *dikē*.[21]

Herodotus's story of Deioces illustrates several features of a properly functioning legal process. First there is need of a judge, or judges. The judge does not need to be outstandingly just, like Deioces, since the system apparently functioned reasonably well before his participation, but without any judge, or with only corrupt judges, the process will not function at all and lawlessness will reign. Secondly, the fact that Deioces put all the other judges out of business shows that in a truly voluntary system the better judges will tend to be selected and the system will thus naturally tend to produce good judges. A similar conclusion can be drawn from the scene on Achilles' shield, where the judge giving "the straightest *dikē*" is rewarded with two talents of gold. This prize is a powerful incentive for the judges to pronounce straight *dikai*. In other words, the system ought to favor good judges and thus to produce the kind of judges necessary to keep it functioning well. Only when a judge or group of judges gains exclusive control of the system, as the kings in Hesiod's village seem to have done, can they become lazy or corrupt and still retain their positions.

A properly functioning system also requires honest pleas from

20. "Do not settle a case before hearing both sides" (Hesiod, frag. 338); cf. Aeschylus, *Eu.* 428.

21. One might think of such a system as "pure procedural justice," as defined by Rawls: "Pure procedural justice obtains when there is no independent criterion for the right result: instead there is a correct or fair procedure such that the outcome is likewise correct or fair, whatever it is, provided that the procedure has been properly followed" (1971, 86).

the litigants, and here too the Greek system favors the desired end. Litigants who agree to submit their disputes for settlement are likely to have at least a partially valid claim; an utter scoundrel will simply avoid the system. In a small community, moreover, people pleading in a public forum can hardly falsify significant facts. And in the disputes we have examined, where the facts are seldom in question and the dispute concerns primarily honor or status, a settlement depends more on the litigants' honest desire to settle than on their speaking the truth about the facts of the matter. Thus the litigants who use the process will be already disposed to reach a settlement and abide by it, and the temptation to speak falsely will be minimized.

The public nature of the procedure, moreover, allows public opinion to become a powerful force that can put pressure on the judges to render fair settlements and on the litigants to use the process and to accept those settlements. As far as we can tell, there was no means of enforcing settlements other than by self-help, and enforcement would be unnecessary at this stage if both the litigants accepted the settlement. This is not to say that all litigants actually adhered to settlements they had accepted. Hesiod says that he and Perses had already divided their inheritance when Perses tried to carry off more than his share (WD 37–39), and this was surely not the only case in which a publicly accepted settlement (if that is what it was) did not end a dispute.[22] But under a properly functioning system of voluntary submission of disputes for settlement the enforcement of settlements ought to be a relatively minor problem.

We may assume, however, that the system did not always work well. In actual practice the competitive values of the Greeks may have led many of them to resort to force or the threat of force rather than look for a peaceful settlement. The literary evidence suggests that the leaders of society could to some extent ignore the pressure of public opinion, but presumably others were more susceptible to such pressure. Other problems are indicated by Hesiod's continual complaints about kings who hand down crooked settlements or litigants who plead crookedly or swear false oaths. Clearly the system does not guarantee either wise judges or honest litigants, and it may

---

22. Anthropologists are now tending to see dispute settlement as a continuing process (or "extended case"), in which a particular settlement is not the end of a dispute but only a stage in a long-term relation between the disputing parties; see van Velsen 1967 and Nader in Nader and Todd 1978, 8.

sometimes have happened that, in Hesiod's words, "The more un-just man receives the larger settlement." [23] Although we must not be misled by Hesiod, whose generally sour attitude toward life may have led him to distort the actual situation,[24] it would not be impos-sible for a corrupt or stupid judge to be established, especially if the judicial process came to be controlled by a small group of nobles or "kings," as Hesiod implies. And as the population increased and more cases were submitted for settlement, it could easily be that second-rate judges would need to be enlisted, thereby endangering the proper functioning of the whole system. We can only speculate, but it is possible that such a situation had been reached in some areas at the time of the earliest written laws.

The enactment of written laws in the seventh and sixth centuries resulted in some obvious changes, especially in the area of proce-dural justice. As far as we can tell, however, the substantive element in early written laws in large part reaffirmed traditional customs, though some lawgivers, notably Solon, also enacted laws to cover situations that had not previously been subject to any rule.[25] The clearest surviving example of substantive continuity is Draco's homicide law, which preserves the same basic penalties of exile and compensation for homicide as we find in the Homeric poems, while removing some of the ambiguity concerning the appropriate com-pensation (restitution or retribution) that existed in earlier times. In another area, Solon's law allowing a man to make a will and adopt an heir, though apparently a new idea, applied only to men who had no natural sons; thus the law did not disturb, and indeed im-plicitly reaffirmed, the most fundamental rule of the traditional sys-tem of inheritance, that a man's natural son inherits his estate. Simi-larly, Charondas's fixing of finely differentiated penalties for various offenses probably did not significantly change the kinds of wrongs for which men were penalized but rather made a judge's determina-

23. μείζω γε δίκην ἀδικώτερος ἕξει (*WD* 272); the play between "more unjust" (*adikōteros*) and "settlement" (*dikē*) is untranslatable.

24. Although Hesiod complains vociferously of being a victim of the judicial pro-cess, it appears that he is in fact quite well off, whereas Perses appears to be quite poor; see Gagarin 1974. Note also that Hesiod gives an extremely negative picture of the land of Ascra, which in fact is quite a pleasant and fertile place; see Wallace 1974. It is possible that Hesiod's bitterness is just a part of his poetic persona, as Griffith 1983 argues.

25. I can find no precedent in earlier customs, for example, for Solon's law re-stricting exports (F 65).

tion of the penalty for a specific wrong more straightforward and consistent.

In all these areas the lawgivers seem to have followed traditional customs fairly closely; nonetheless, the transition from unwritten customs to written laws did produce some significant changes. In enacting written laws the lawgivers must have attempted to resolve and eliminate any vagueness, ambiguity, or conflict present in the traditional rules and customs. Although no written code will ever be wholly without contradictions or ambiguity, even very general written laws are normally more precise than orally preserved customs. Writing undoubtedly made possible a greater precision, and the early Greek lawgivers apparently took advantage of this, since they clearly enacted some rather precise laws.[26]

Subsequent legislation could be written, moreover, to eliminate ambiguities or otherwise overcome difficulties that had become evident in the implementation of the laws enacted earlier.[27] In many cases changes were made in the form of amendments that preserved the letter of the earlier written text while sometimes significantly altering its application.[28] Of course, in attempting to remove the ambiguities present in the traditional customs and to set fixed, consistent, and appropriate penalties for precisely defined wrongs, the lawgivers tended, perhaps unintentionally, to make the laws considerably more complex, particularly in areas like inheritance,[29] though the basic substantive rules and principles of the past remained fairly constant.

In addition to these evident changes, the enactment of substantive laws must in itself have had an important effect on the functioning of the legal system and on the authority of law in the community. By setting precise penalties for different offenses, written

26. The story that Solon's laws were intentionally ambiguous probably arose long after he enacted them; see *Ath. Pol.* 9.2 with Rhodes 1981, ad loc., and Plutarch, *Sol.* 18.4. There is no evidence that Solon himself made this claim.

27. The Great Code at Gortyn gives some insight into this historical process. The first section, for example, contains first (1.2–12) the general rule of procedure to be followed (see p. 96 above). This is followed by more precise, supplementary provisions (1.12–2.2), which, I have argued (Gagarin 1982, 138–40), were enacted at a later time.

28. See Gagarin 1981a, 21–29, and 1982.

29. The Gortyn Law Code (*IC* 4.72) probably represents the end of a gradual process of increasing elaboration of the inheritance laws, which occupy more than a third of this large inscription.

legislation removed some (though by no means all) of the discretion of judges and juries and made the procedure more certain for the litigants, less adaptable to differences among individual litigants, and ultimately fairer in most cases. In a small preliterate community, as we have seen, settlements tend to be ad hoc and to vary with the status of the litigants. Written laws can at least reduce some of the diversity of settlements in similar cases. There is a loss, of course, in the reduced flexibility of written laws; despite concessions to the principle of equity, the letter of the law often cannot adequately take into consideration all significant factors. Even before the advent of written laws, as the Greek communities grew larger, it was probably becoming more difficult to maintain a system flexible enough to adapt its rules fairly to each dispute, and written laws probably just hastened the trend toward less personal legal settlements. Thus, written, substantive laws in themselves reduced the power of magistrates and increased the power and authority of the legal system, and ultimately of the polis itself, in regulating the behavior of its inhabitants.

These trends are even more evident in the procedural legislation enacted during the period. The most important general procedural development was the trend toward compulsory prosecution in place of the voluntary submission of disputes to a judicial body for settlement. Not that voluntary arbitration ever died out; even in the fourth century voluntary, private arbitration was an important Athenian institution,[30] and in the *Laws* (767B) Plato recommends that "the most authoritative (*kyriōtaton*)[31] court should be where the parties together choose the jurors and plead their own cases themselves." But compulsory procedures clearly became widespread during the archaic period.

The change from voluntary to compulsory procedure was probably gradual and complex. As we have seen in Chapter 2 above, even in preliterate times the submission of a dispute for settlement was not entirely voluntary, in that the pressure of public opinion and the preference for a peaceful settlement undoubtedly constrained the disputants to some extent. Over a period of time, moreover, the repeated use of legal institutions for the peaceful settle-

---

30. See MacDowell 1978, 203–11.

31. There is some uncertainty about the sense of this word and of the whole passage; see England 1921, on 767B2.

ment of disputes would establish de facto precedents, which would be increasingly difficult to ignore, provided that the settlements were generally perceived as fair. By the time of the earliest written legislation the use of judges or courts for dispute settlement was well established, and we should perhaps talk less of a single point of transition to compulsory procedure than of a gradual strengthening and extension of the power of courts and judges.

During this transition from voluntary to compulsory procedure, however, there must have been a point at which one disputant, instead of having to rely on his own persuasiveness or the force of public opinion, could employ some public means to compel his opponent to submit their dispute for settlement. As Wolff has written:

> It would be contrary to human nature to suppose that even the strongest pressure of public opinion alone could ever effectively eliminate the use of force and bring about a satisfactory system of law and order by inducing litigants to seek peaceful arbitration and abide by the awards. We have no reason to assume that a tendency toward arbitration in primitive society should have been any more successful in suppressing anarchy than were similar efforts in modern international relations.[32]

Assuming this view is correct, at what precise point did the submission of a dispute for judgment become truly compulsory, and how was this achieved?

As we saw in Chapter 2, there is abundant evidence that in preliterate Greece disputes were submitted for settlement voluntarily. The earliest document presenting clear evidence for a system of compulsory legal procedure is Draco's homicide law. As far as we can tell from the preserved inscription, this law contained no explicit statement that, when summoned, a person must appear in court but rather treated the matter indirectly. The law states that the victim's relatives are to make a proclamation, presumably identifying the alleged killer by name, and are to proceed with the prosecution.[33] The killer then has three choices: he may go immediately into exile, thereby in effect acknowledging his guilt and probably allowing the relatives to obtain a pronouncement of his guilt from the

32. Wolff 1946, 32–33. The traditional view of a gradual transition to compulsory litigation, which Wolff is here challenging, is most fully articulated by Steinwenter 1925; see Harrison 1971, 69–72 for a summary of the dispute.

33. Lines 20–23. For the text of Draco's law see chap. 4 above.

court; he may submit to a trial, in which case he will be indirectly protected by the polis[34] until the trial, as long as he observes rules excluding him from most public and sacred places; or finally he may ignore the proclamation. In this last case he could be killed immediately or summarily arrested (by *apagōgē*) if he enters any public or sacred place, and if he does not appear in court he will probably be convicted of the homicide in absentia and may then be killed or summarily arrested with impunity by anyone anywhere in Athenian territory.[35] In this way the power of the community is formally, though indirectly, brought to bear on the killer to submit to a trial.

Although strictly speaking an accused killer is not explicitly forced to stand trial, I think we can legitimately designate this a system of compulsory prosecution, since the net effect is that the accused killer must stand trial if he wishes to remain freely in Attica, and the accusing relative must bring the case to trial if he wishes to punish the killer without suffering in return. Both litigants, moreover, would have to follow the procedure set forth in the law. This system thus appears to be significantly different from the pre-Draconian situation,[36] where an accused killer could not be free to

34. The protection afforded the killer by the polis probably took the form of refusing to recognize the right of anyone to harm the killer, unless he was caught in one of the public places from which the initial proclamation barred him. This provision may have occupied all or part of the gap (lines 23–26) before the provision protecting killers in exile. We hear of no special sanctuaries for alleged killers in early times, and by the terms of Draco's law they would be barred from those sanctuaries where other suppliants might seek protection.

35. For details concerning the use of *apagōgē* in homicide cases, see Hansen 1976, 99–108, Gagarin 1979, and Hansen 1981. For speculation on the origin of the procedure see p. 22, n. 9, above. I assume that Draco's law made the procedure of *apagōgē* available for anyone, not just relatives of the victim. Lines 30–31 probably stated that "it is allowed to kill or arrest (*apagein*) killers, if they are caught in the territory [of Athens]," and the absence of qualification probably implies that it was allowed for anyone. Hansen (1976, 115) observes that since Aristotle attributes the introduction of public prosecution by all citizens to Solon (*Ath. Pol.* 9.1; see chap. 3 above), Draco's law probably restricted the use of *apagōgē* to relatives of the victim, but Aristotle is probably thinking of the *graphē*, not the much less common procedure of *apagōgē*. On the other hand, it is possible that *apagōgē* against accused or convicted killers was in practice employed only by relatives of the victim, and it is perhaps significant that whereas the *graphē* explicitly allows "anyone who wishes" (ἐξεῖναι τῷ βουλομένῳ) to use the procedure, the provision for *apagōgē* merely allows (ἐξεῖναι) the procedure to be used.

36. I am assuming that before Draco's law the treatment of homicide was more or less the same as we find in the early literature; see Gagarin 1981a, 5–21.

remain in Attica unless he could persuade the relatives to settle the matter either privately or in court, a process entailing some risk of harm from an angry relative. And the victim's relatives would, before Draco, have to rely on their own strength to insure punishment of the killer. Compulsory procedure thus represented a significant advantage for both sides.

Under Draco's law, however, the compulsion is only indirect, since the polis is not yet strong enough directly to compel litigants by means, say, of a police force to use public procedures, nor does it execute sentences.[37] Being indirect, the system is also quite complex. Indeed it is so complex that it seems unlikely that it could have been implemented without written laws, though certain steps may have been taken before the enactment of written legislation. It may have been traditional, for instance, that an alleged killer awaiting trial would not be killed and that anyone who did kill an alleged killer before or during a trial would be treated just like an ordinary killer; but even if such traditional customs were generally accepted, they would undoubtedly contain such a degree of ambiguity or uncertainty that an accused killer could not feel confident in relying on them.

Precisely this sort of situation seems to be reflected in the story of the Cylonian conspiracy in Athens about a decade before the enactment of Draco's laws, if we can trust Plutarch's information that the Cylonians, who had failed in their attempted forceful takeover of the city, were lured away from the sanctuary on the Acropolis, where they had taken refuge, by the promise of a trial and then were killed without any trial.[38] This story illustrates the dangers inherent in this sort of informal procedure in which the two parties agree to a trial. To be sure, written regulations can be violated too, but the provision of clear penalties for violations, usually found in written laws, would make it more difficult to avoid the consequences of a violation. And the need for precise procedural details, such as the list of places the accused killer must avoid in order to insure his protection,[39] would seem to require written legislation and to make it

37. See Gagarin 1981a, 117. Even in fourth-century Athens there were only a few procedures in which the defendant would be forcibly brought to trial by a public official or a sentence would be executed by the state.

38. Plutarch, *Solon* 12.1; neither Herodotus (5.71) nor Thucydides (1.126) mentions the offer of a trial.

39. Cf. the list in Draco's law (lines 26–29) of places the killer in exile must avoid.

virtually impossible to implement an effective system of indirect compulsory procedure without the use of writing.

We can only speculate about the treatment of homicide in Athens before Draco, but it seems likely that the procedural rules we find in Draco's law, though perhaps in general conformity with traditional practices, are new in their specific details. As I have suggested elsewhere,[40] the innovation implied by the provision for retroactive rules for pardon probably lies in the detailed list of relatives and other citizens who may grant pardon, presumably in return for compensation. The idea of pardon being granted by relatives was not new, but Draco's law clarifies precisely who may grant it. Similarly, the lists of precise degrees of relationship in the regulations concerning the proclamation and the prosecution, and of places an exile must avoid, though probably conforming in general to traditional practices, are unlikely to have been either formulated or observed in practice with any degree of precision before they were set down explicitly in writing. All these considerations point to the conclusion that the point of transition to a truly compulsory system of legal procedure was the introduction of written laws, which allowed the specification of detail necessary for the operation of the system we have outlined above.

Thus Draco's homicide law, by its elaboration of procedural details, established the necessary involvement of the traditional court in the settlement of homicide cases. Although the law did not eliminate the need for self-help, it reduced the role of self-help to a relatively few, well-defined situations,[41] and even in these cases the law allowed people a choice between extrajudicial self-help and self-help within the system. In other words, the court may sentence a killer to exile, but it is the task of the victim's relatives (or any other concerned citizen) to see that this sentence is obeyed, either by taking direct physical action against the killer or by the public procedure of *apagōgē*. In this way Draco's law combines a basically compulsory procedure with elements of the traditional system of voluntary self-help, thereby setting the pattern for Athenian law for centuries to come.[42]

40. Gagarin 1981a, 54.

41. See Gagarin 1981a, esp. 162–64.

42. Hansen 1976, 114 notes that self-help by means of *apagōgē* could be used in the same situations in the fourth century as in earlier times. It is possible, however, that in practice its use had diminished considerably.

The advent of compulsory procedure undoubtedly contributed to increased use of the legal process. Moreover, although some of the early laws concerning commercial transactions were apparently intended to reduce the use of the judicial process,[43] most laws setting precisely graded penalties for crimes or prescribing elaborate rules of inheritance probably led to the greater use of courts, even if such was not their intent. This expanded use of the courts in turn led to a more elaborate notion of due process, as can be seen in the many procedural innovations of the period whose intent was apparently to make the legal system work more fairly.

Access to the courts was expanded by the creation of new forms of procedure that made it easier in many cases to bring someone to court: particularly significant are the Athenian procedures of *apagōgē, graphē*, and *eisangelia*. The creation and expansion of these and other procedures increased the complexity of early Greek procedural law and led to the situation we find in classical Athens, where in many cases several different procedures were available to someone wanting to prosecute a particular offense.[44] More important, the availability of so many procedures had the predictable effect, at least in Athens, of an even greater increase in the use of the courts, so that by the end of the fifth century the city was thought by many to be overrun with lawsuits and courts.[45]

The notion of due process also seems to have inspired laws requiring that proper notice be given of one's intent to bring a suit. Draco's homicide law requires that the victim's relatives publicly proclaim their intent to prosecute, and Charondas created the new procedure of *episkēpsis*, which begins with the formal notification of intent to prosecute.

A concern for due process is also evident in various attempts to provide greater help in the enforcement of settlements. Traditionally enforcement had been left to self-help, and there were undoubtedly cases in which a litigant would find it difficult or impossible to recover what he had been awarded by a court. In a voluntary system such cases would be relatively rare, since both litigants would usually accept the settlement, but with the growth of compulsory pro-

43. See chap. 3 above.
44. For examples see Hansen 1976, 120.
45. Cf. the stock Aristophanic joke (e.g., *Clouds* 207–8): "This can't be Athens; I don't see any law courts." There are those who would argue that the United States is currently moving toward a similar situation.

cedure it would more often be the case that the losing party to a dispute would be unwilling to accept the final settlement and would seek to avoid his obligations.

Several different means of assisting litigants in the enforcement of settlements were tried. Early laws at Eretria and Gortyn seek to remedy this by requiring certain magistrates to enforce settlements and fining those who do not, and the Eretrian law also prescribes exile for anyone not paying a fine.[46] Solon's remedy was different; his *dikē exoulēs* allowed anyone who could not recover what was owed him after a settlement to bring another suit, and this time the penalty would be doubled. Another method of enforcement is found in the first section of the Great Code at Gortyn, where fines are prescribed for anyone who does not give up a disputed person within five days after being ordered to do so by a court.[47] Although the Greeks never developed entirely adequate means of enforcing judicial settlements,[48] this area clearly saw considerable expansion in the procedural law of the archaic period.

In addition to expanding the scope of procedural law the written legislation of the archaic period also was concerned with the precision of certain formal aspects of procedure, in particular the use of oaths and witnesses in a trial. Judging from the literary evidence we examined in Chapter 2, it appears that although oaths formed a regular part of preliterate judicial procedure and witnesses were probably also employed in some cases, the rules governing the use of oaths and witnesses were not precisely formulated, as they are in the early written laws. In particular, the notion that a certain specific number of witnesses can determine the outcome of a case, which we find in several of the regulations of the Great Code at Gortyn and in the early homicide law from Cumae, was probably something new. It may have been traditional before the advent of written laws to bring a certain number of witnesses in certain kinds of cases, but there is no indication (and it seems in itself unlikely) that neglect of a formal requirement, such as a failure to have the required

46. The laws from Eretria and Gortyn (*IC* 4.14.*g–p*.1) are discussed in chap. 4 above.
47. *IC* 4.72.1.24–39. I have argued elsewhere (Gagarin 1982, 139–40) that this provision was probably enacted later than the basic law concerning disputed possession (for which see chap. 4 above) but earlier than the final inscription of the Code.
48. On Demosthenes' difficulties in recovering a court-awarded judgment, see p. 74, n. 101, above.

four witnesses, could cause someone to lose a case, until the number became precisely fixed by a written law. Here too the written laws probably made the judicial system less flexible, and this innovation, together with the elaboration of procedural details observable, for example, in Draco's homicide law, suggests that early written legislation introduced a degree of formalism into Greek legal procedure that was not present earlier.[49]

Finally, there is a definite tendency during this period to limit the power of individual magistrates in the judicial process. Formal restrictions mandating a certain verdict if certain requirements concerning oaths or witnesses are met were one limitation by written laws on the presiding magistrate's power.[50] The setting of precise penalties may also have been intended to do this, though it is not certain that such laws would actually have this effect, since a judge might still have the power to determine the precise nature of a wrong, thereby determining the penalty. Two other kinds of laws, however, those limiting a judicial magistrate's tenure in office (as at Dreros) and those providing for the appeal of a magistrate's decision (as at Chios or Athens), clearly limited their power. And although we do not know what kind of cases were tried by juries, Charondas's requirement that all citizens serve on juries would have further reduced the power of individual magistrates.

These procedural reforms seem to have been intended primarily to make the judicial system function more fairly. It is difficult to say whether they increased the power of any political group in the polis, since we do not know precisely how any of these laws functioned. Solon's laws, for example, appeared to Aristotle as "democratic," but it is by no means certain that this was their intent, and "the people" did not in fact gain much political power until nearly a century later, after a long period of tyrannical rule. Similarly, the Chian inscription seems to give power to a popular body, but in fact the government of Chios remained aristocratic long after this reform.[51]

49. The common assumption that the formalism of primitive law gradually diminishes in legal systems is derived primarily from the evidence of Roman law. It does not seem valid for Greece, or for most of the primitive cultures studied by anthropologists; cf., however, Gernet 1968, 217–47.

50. The laws on the Great Code at Gortyn (*IC* 4.72) direct the judge in some cases to judge the dispute himself on oath and in others to render a decision in accordance with a specific number of witnesses or certain specific testimony. Clearly the latter approach restricted the judge's power to decide cases on his own judgment.

51. See p. 91, n. 28, above.

We shall examine the political effects of written laws at greater length in the next chapter.

The expansion and development of legal procedure during the archaic period clearly had the overall effect of increasing the use of and access to the legal process and of limiting the power of individuals to resort to self-help and of magistrates to make arbitrary or corrupt decisions. The evidence indicates clearly that, although the earliest written laws included numerous substantive provisions, the primary concern of legislation during the period was to make the judicial process fairer, more effective, more widely available, and more widely used. To judge from the situation in Athens, this goal was in large part attained, though naturally with the increasing use of the system came new problems, which are beyond the scope of the present work. In the next chapter I shall consider the reasons for the emergence of law in Greece during the archaic period.

6

THE EMERGENCE OF WRITTEN LAW

We have seen that formal procedures for settling disputes were well established in Greece before the introduction of writing around the middle of the eighth century. We have also seen that Greek cities began to write down laws about the middle of the seventh century and that by the end of the sixth century many cities had some written laws.[1] Before we try to account for the widespread appearance of written laws throughout Greece during the last half of the archaic period, let us first examine various reasons other scholars have suggested.

Perhaps the most commonly accepted view explains the writing down of laws as part of a political struggle by the people for relief from the arbitrary power of their aristocratic rulers. As Bury-Meiggs put it,

> There can be no assurance that equal justice will be meted out to all, so long as the laws by which the judge is supposed to act are not accessible to all. A written code of laws is a condition of just judgement, however just the laws themselves may be. It was therefore natural that one of the first demands the people in Greek cities pressed upon their aristocratic governments, and one of the first concessions those governments were forced to make was a written law.[2]

1. I am not concerned to establish just how many cities had written laws by, say, 500 B.C. Ruschenbusch (1983) argues that most Greek poleis were small and that only the larger ones, perhaps 100 out of 700, had written laws. Although our evidence is hardly sufficient to decide the matter, Ruschenbusch may be right that small cities would have less need of written laws, and some may have managed without them. Against Ruschenbusch one might argue that the lawgiver of a small polis would not be long remembered, and that even if a small polis relied largely on the laws of a larger polis, it may have reinscribed or somehow officially recognized them. Even if Ruschenbusch is correct, moreover, it is still important to investigate the reasons for the enactment of written legislation in most of the larger cities.

2. Bury-Meiggs 1975, 104; cf. Bonner and Smith 1930, 67, and Calhoun 1944, 20–21. Glotz (1904, 239–43) argues that the earliest written laws were the judg-

The words of Theseus in Euripides' *Suppliants* (produced ca. 420 B.C.) are often cited in connection with this view: "When laws are written down, the poor and the rich have equal justice" (433–34). This explanation has a certain initial plausibility, and we know that several of the early lawgivers were appointed during times of civic turmoil. As a general account of the origin of written laws, however, it is open to a number of serious objections.

First, the theory rests on the assumption that before laws are written down, they exist and are transmitted in the form of oral rules. As we saw in Chapter 1, however, people do not normally have a separate group of rules that function as laws before the advent of writing. Certainly the Greeks did not have "oral laws" before they had written laws. Indeed the idea of "unwritten law" does not appear in Greece until the fifth century, long after the enactment of written laws,[3] and the very notion of unwritten law is probably impossible without knowledge of writing. The demand (if such it was) for written laws, therefore, could not have arisen from a desire to have a certain group of "laws" written down which had hitherto been unwritten.

Nor is there evidence that before the lawgivers any body of rules, whether oral or written, was under the exclusive control of one group in the society. Although judicial procedure was in the hands of various aristocratic groups in different cities, there is no evidence that, in the words of Sir Henry Maine, "What the juristical oligarchy . . . claims is to monopolise the *knowledge* of the laws, to have the exclusive possession of the principles by which quarrels are decided."[4] Hesiod complains of the crookedness of both kings and litigants but never suggests that the traditional rules were inaccessible or that greater accessibility to certain rules would be desirable. In fact, Hesiod seems not to have any idea that there is a body of unwritten rules which could be written down to serve as laws. The only possible evidence for privately known rules is Aristotle's state-

---

ments handed down in previous decisions of courts; the kings who judged cases could distort these earlier rulings (according to Glotz) and so the people demanded they be recorded. Cf. also Gerner's view that the development of Athenian law was the result of two conflicting tendencies, the growth of the sovereignty of the polis and the desire for individual freedom from state control; the latter tendency (he argues) first manifests itself in the writing down of laws (Gerner 1950, esp. 21).

3. The earliest reference to unwritten laws is in Antigone's famous speech; see p. 55, n. 13, above.

4. Maine 1861, 7.

ment that the Athenian *thesmothetai* "wrote down early *thesmia* and kept them for the deciding of disputes."[5] But Aristotle implies that these *thesmia* were publicly recorded, and the one likely example of such a *thesmion*, the rule in *Ath. Pol.* 16.10 that anyone seeking to establish a tyranny will be outlawed, is hardly likely to have been kept secret from the people of Athens.

The assumption, moreover, that the earliest lawgivers simply recorded in writing rules previously preserved only orally by the ruling classes, who controlled the judicial process in part by their control of the preservation and transmission of these oral rules, runs counter to much of the evidence. Although many of the substantive laws of early Greece may have preserved traditional customs, we noted some significant substantive innovations, and more importantly in the area of procedural law, which was apparently of greater concern to the early lawgivers, innovation was common. Indeed, the clear purpose of most of the procedural laws was to change various aspects of existing procedure. There is hardly any evidence, in other words, to support the view that the early Greek lawgivers took rules previously controlled by a small group and by writing them down made them available to everyone.

Second, there is no evidence from this period for the sentiment that written laws are in themselves fairer or more just than unwritten laws, or whatever is imagined to precede written laws. There is considerable evidence in the early inscriptions, for example, that reform of the legal system was an important and widespread concern; as we have seen, different cities approached the matter of reform in different ways. Nowhere, however, do we find any suggestion that the writing down of laws is part of this reform or is in itself desirable. And the democratic (or potentially democratic) reforms of the period, though they may have taken the form of written laws, have nothing to do with the writing down of laws per se.

As we have noted, the equation of written laws with justice first appears in the fifth century, and it may be, as Thomas has argued, that "although written codes were a precondition for the eventual perception of inequities, such a perception was surely the result, not the cause, of the codification."[6] According to Thomas, the writing down of laws significantly alters people's way of thinking about their rules of behavior. "Given this altered mentality, brought about by

5. *Ath. Pol.* 3.4; see p. 51, n.2, above.
6. Thomas 1977, 455.

the spread of literacy, social, political and economic inequities could be perceived; then, but only then, could pressure for reform grow among 'the people.'"[7] This argument raises many important questions about written and oral communication and their consequences that lie beyond the scope of my investigation, but it is certainly possible that a concern for "justice" (in some sense of the term) was an effect rather than the cause of written laws.

A third objection is that there is little evidence for the widespread expression of popular or democratic sentiment in archaic Greece; certainly such feelings do not appear to have been strong enough to cause most Greek cities to write down their laws by the end of the sixth century.[8] And in fact the legislation of the early lawgivers was not particularly democratic, but was enacted by governments that were, for the most part, aristocratic or even tyrannical at the time of the legislation and remained so long afterwards.[9] This is true even in Chios, where a sixth-century law included the potentially democratic institution of appeal to a popular council and yet apparently did not alter the basically aristocratic nature of government on the island.[10] Even Solon's laws (not the first to be written in Athens), though they later evolved into strongly democratic reforms, were at the time seen as holding to a middle course between the upper and lower classes.[11] During the sixth century democracy developed slowly in a few cities, notably Athens, though only at the very end of the century; in most, however, aristocracy or tyranny prevailed. Certainly written laws did not stimulate a widespread democratic movement, and it seems hardly likely that they were inspired by the hope for such a movement.

Nor can we trace a demand for written laws to any other single

7. Ibid., 458. Cf. the interesting theory proposed by Calhoun, who suggests that with the writing down of laws "changes become distinctly perceptible, and when made have to be made consciously and intentionally. . . . And so begins a long process which matures in a fully developed system of statute law, with permanent legislative machinery and provisions for periodic revision, and gradually transforms the esoteric legal lore of the aristocracy into legal science" (1944, 22–23).

8. Cf. Thomas 1977, 455–56.

9. Cf., for example, Graham: "[Zaleucus's] apparent aim of creating a strongly disciplined society ruled by unchanging laws seems well suited to the oligarchic constitution that we know at Locri" (1982, 191).

10. See Forrest's remark cited p. 91, n. 28, above.

11. See Aristotle, *Ath. Pol.* 11.2 and the poems of Solon cited in *Ath. Pol.* 12 (i.e., frags. 5, 6, 34, 36, 37 West = 5, 23, 24, 25 Diehl).

political group, such as dissident aristocrats or antityrannical parties.[12] Although it is often said that a written code of laws ultimately puts a check on absolute power,[13] the evidence from early Greek history makes this assertion at least questionable. Judicial magistrates may have less autonomy once laws are written, but absolute political power may remain unchecked, as it did in a number of Greek cities. The long history of Near-Eastern law codes, which coexisted for centuries with strongly monarchical governments, provides further evidence, though, as we shall see below, the legal nature of these Near-Eastern codes is problematic. These Near-Eastern law codes were apparently intended to increase the authority of the king by demonstrating the justness of his reign and increasing the public's awareness of his administration.[14] They did nothing to strengthen the power of the people, nor was that their intent.

In any case, there is no evidence that the earliest Greek lawgivers viewed their laws as a restraint on absolute power, and the fact that at least one of them, Pittacus, was widely regarded as a tyrant himself appears to rule out the possibility that the Greeks themselves held the view that written laws would help prevent the accumulation of power by one person or a small group of people. We should note, moreover, that even in Athens the publication of written laws did not prevent the establishment of Pisistratus's tyranny not long after Solon's reforms, and that Pisistratus himself apparently felt no need to change or abolish the laws of Solon and Draco but rather continued to observe them while he ruled.[15] We have seen that the written laws of early Greece gave individual magistrates less control over the judicial process and increased the role of legal procedure at the expense of traditional means of self-help. To the extent that the government of a particular polis, such as Athens, later became more

12. This seems to be the view presented by Snodgrass 1980, 118–22. Cf. Andrewes: "Publication of the law [sc. of Draco] was a curtailment of aristocratic privilege" (1982, 370).

13. See, e.g., Snodgrass 1980, 118–19.

14. See Whitelam 1979, 17–37 and see below.

15. The main sources are Herodotus 1.59.6 and Thucydides 6.54.6. *Ath. Pol.* 22.1 reports that Peisistratus did not use Solon's laws, but this appears to be contradicted by *Ath. Pol.* 16.8 (see Rhodes 1981, ad loc.). Other sources (including *Ath. Pol.* 16.8) relate that Peisistratus even obeyed a summons to appear before the Areopagus on a charge of homicide, though his accusor failed to appear; see Andrewes 1982, 406 for further references. Even if Solon's laws were maintained, however, we do not know just how they functioned in practice during the tyranny.

democratic, these legal reforms may have later increased the power of the people. But initially the laws seemed designed to benefit the whole polis and thus to strengthen the control of whatever group already governed the city, and at the time the ruling parties were virtually all aristocratic.

In sum, the call for a lawgiver in a time of internal crisis was a call for significantly (though not entirely) new laws rather than for the mere recording of previously existing rules. In some cities the publication of laws may sooner or later have served the purpose of strengthening the hand of the people, but in other cities it may have had very different effects. On the basis of the evidence we can only conclude that it is very unlikely that the demand for equal justice for all was a significant reason, let alone the main inspiration, for any of the earliest written laws in Greece.

We may dispense more quickly with a variation of the view that written laws were a democratic development, namely the theory that codification was connected with the needs of trade, which was controlled by the aristocracy until the merchant class began to seek a greater role.[16] Increase in trade was certainly one of the features of the rapid economic development that occurred during this period, but trade can hardly have been the primary reason for writing down laws. Except for a few of Solon's laws we find almost no laws concerning trade in the earliest codes, and even the extensive mid-fifth-century code at Gortyn says almost nothing explicitly about trade. It is hard to see how there could be any close connection between trade and the writing down of laws.

A third theory attributes the inspiration for written laws to Near-Eastern influence:

> The strong probability of actual settlements of Semitic craftsmen in Crete between the late ninth and seventh centuries . . . could well mean that the Near East helped to familiarize the Archaic Cretans with the concept of a written code.[17]

16. See Willetts: "There appears to be a marked connection between trade, coinage and written law on an extensive scale" (1967, 9). This view is repeated in Willetts 1974, 27 and Willetts 1982, 240. Willetts also suggests (1974, 25–26) that Cretan laws may go back to Minoan laws. No evidence survives, however, for law in Minoan times, and its existence is quite doubtful.

17. Jeffery 1976, 189; the fullest statement of this view is by Boardman 1970, 23, who relies on the work of Huxley 1962 (see p. 61, n. 43, above) and Mühl 1933 (see below).

Although the evidence for Semitic crafts (and thus presumably Semitic craftsmen) in Crete at this time is persuasive, there is no evidence that they helped stimulate the writing down of laws. Other objections to this view may also be raised.

First, it is by no means certain that Crete really was the first place where the Greeks wrote down laws. Although the earliest surviving legal inscriptions come from Crete, this may be due to the vagaries of preservation and does not necessarily indicate that these were in fact the earliest laws to be written down. The laws of other cities may have been written on perishable materials rather than stone, as the early Athenian laws probably were,[18] thus decreasing the chances that they would survive until the present. And the tradition that the first lawgivers were Zaleucus and Charondas, both of whom lived in western colonies far from Crete, was widespread in antiquity and can not easily be dismissed. Nor does the story that Zaleucus learned his laws from a Cretan[19] weigh strongly against this tradition, since the traditional mythological picture of the earliest Cretan kings, Minos and Rhadamanthys, as judges could easily have inspired the chauvinistic story that Zaleucus came under Cretan influence.[20]

As we shall see below, the Cretan cities do not appear to have followed the pattern of single, large-scale legislation common in the rest of Greece. Rather, they apparently enacted and inscribed laws individually or in small groups over a long period. It seems unlikely, therefore, that the Cretan laws could have inspired the writing down of large codes of laws in other cities. It is not impossible that Greek laws were first written down in Crete and that the idea of written laws was then taken over by other cities in the form of large-

18. The laws of Draco and Solon were probably first written on wooden *axōnes* and then on bronze *kyrbeis*, or steles (which would presumably be melted down and reused at a later period). Only at the end of the fifth century did the Athenians inscribe these laws on stone; see Stroud 1979, 41–44 and passim, and cf. Jeffery 1961a, 58–59.

19. Aristotle, *Pol.* 1274A25–31, whom Jeffery and others cite, dismisses the story of Cretan influence, which is clearly inconsistent with his description of Zaleucus's activity (frag. 548; see chap. 3 above).

20. It is unlikely that the mythological account of Minos and Rhadamanthys was influenced by the (possible) historical fact that Crete was the first place to have written laws, since the mythological tradition is attested for Minos, at least, as early as the *Odyssey* (11.568–71; see chap. 2 above).

scale legislation, but it seems somewhat more likely that other cities first enacted written laws earlier than those in Crete or independent of Cretan influence.

Second, even if the earliest Greek laws were recorded in cities in Crete, this does not mean they were inspired by Near-Eastern influence. There is little evidence of any direct connection between the content of Near-Eastern law codes and that of early Greek laws, certainly not enough to indicate that the idea of written laws came from the Orient.

In a thorough survey of possible connections between Near-Eastern and early Greek laws, Mühl[21] claims to find direct oriental influence in a variety of Greek laws: the *lex talionis* of Zaleucus, a law of Gortyn providing compensation to an adopted son who has been rejected, Charondas's law prohibiting sales on credit, Solon's laws prohibiting enslavement for debt and distinguishing between theft at night and theft during the day, and a few others. But even if we accept Mühl's claim that these laws really are similar to various Near-Eastern laws, his claim of direct influence is doubtful. It is highly unlikely that these different lawgivers from all over the Greek world were aware of and influenced by Near-Eastern codes from several different times and places. In all these cases one may more easily explain the apparent similarity between two laws as natural solutions to common problems.[22]

We should note, moreover, an important difference between Near-Eastern codes and the early Greek laws. Whereas the latter are heavily devoted to procedural matters, the Near-Eastern codes show almost no concern with procedure.[23] Thus the Near-Eastern codes cannot have inspired the early Greek lawgivers in this very signifi-

21. Mühl 1933; see also chap. 3 above. Mühl draws his parallels from many different Near-Eastern codes, most of which are centuries older than the Greek laws and were not in force during the time the Greeks were enacting laws.

22. Another possible connection between Near-Eastern codes and Cretan laws is proposed by Pounder 1984, who argues that the puzzling letters near the beginning of the earliest Dreros law (see p. 82, n. 3, above) should be interpreted to mean "may God destroy him [sc. the one who breaks the law]" (Θιὸς ὄλοι ὄν) and suggests that this curse may be connected with certain apotropaic curses found on Near-Eastern boundary stones, buildings and treaties (but not, apparently, on law codes). I do not find Pounder's argument persuasive.

23. In Hammurabi's law, for example, sections 1–5 are directly concerned with procedure; the remaining sections (6–282) are entirely substantive.

cant area. And even if Near-Eastern influence on a few of the laws of Solon and others could be convincingly demonstrated, this would not mean that the idea of a written law code came to any of the early lawgivers from the Near East.[24]

In these ways (and in others we shall consider below) the differences between Greek and Near-Eastern law codes are greater and more significant than their similarities. We can only conclude that the theory that the Greeks learned about written laws from Near-Eastern craftsmen is just a guess, inspired in part, perhaps, by the common tendency of scholars to attribute every development to some external influence. Although it may be impossible to disprove the theory completely, there is no good reason to accept it. I might add that even if the first Greek laws were written down by a Cretan who had heard about written laws from a Near-Eastern craftsman, this would do nothing to explain the rapid spread of the movement to enact written laws. The widespread appearance of this phenomenon in the Greek world at this time suggests rather that we look to the Greeks themselves for the motivation to begin enacting written laws.

A fourth theory attributes the writing down of laws to the colonizing movement in the eighth and seventh centuries:

> It is only natural that the colonists, freed from the restraints of conservatism at home, should be more progressive and more inclined to embark on social and political reforms. . . . In the Greek colonies, codification was sometimes rendered imperative because the colonists were recruited from different cities with divergent systems of customary law.[25]

This view also appears initially plausible, since new cities might well require a new set of laws and the traditionally earliest lawgivers, Zaleucus and Charondas, legislated for colonial cities.[26] However, many of the earliest written laws were in cities such as Athens or the Cretan cities that were not colonies, and although Zaleucus may have enacted his laws not long after the foundation of

---

24. Solon, of course, had the example of Draco and the other earlier Greek lawgivers.

25. Bonner and Smith 1930, 69.

26. We might add Pythagoras to this group, since he apparently wrote laws for Croton in Southern Italy after immigrating there, though our evidence for this is relatively slight; see the references cited by Szegedy-Maszak 1978, 203, n. 21.

Locri, all other colonial lawgivers were active long after the foundation of their cities.[27] It seems, in fact, that the earliest colonies, all of which were composed of settlers from only one mother city each, continued to use the customs and institutions of their parent city and did not at first feel any need for written laws. Of course, a panhellenic colony, such as Thurii (founded 443 B.C.), would need a set of laws immediately (and these, we are told, were provided by Protagoras), but Thurii was clearly an exception.

If none of these theories can explain the widespread practice of written legislation beginning about a century after the Greeks first learned writing, perhaps a slightly different approach to the problem will prove helpful. We know that once the Greeks learned to write, they began to inscribe a variety of material. At first we find only what we might call "private" inscriptions, such as dedications and graffiti.[28] No public inscriptions have been found older than the middle of the seventh century, and though the evidence is insufficient to draw conclusions with certainty, it appears that the earliest public inscriptions are laws.[29] Thus the writing down of laws and other public documents apparently did not come naturally or automatically once writing became known, but must have stemmed from a conscious desire to make certain material available to the general public in the form of public inscription.

27. The traditional Eusebian date for the foundation of Locri is 679 or 673 and for the laws of Zaleucus 663. There is considerable doubt, however, whether Eusebius's evidence for the date of Zaleucus's laws is trustworthy, and many scholars date his activity somewhat later (e.g., Adcock 1927, 101). Catana was founded before 700 and Charondas almost certainly was active after 650 and probably closer to 600. Pythagoras probably lived in Croton about 200 years after its foundation at the end of the eighth century.

28. Jeffery 1961a, 16–17 lists the earliest surviving inscriptions. Coldstream notes that all the earliest graffiti "are concerned with private life," and that the Dreros law is "the earliest known example of Greek alphabetic writing being pressed into the service of the *polis*" (1977, 301–2). Recent epigraphical evidence is surveyed by Johnston 1983.

29. Jeffery 1961a, 58–63 surveys the subjects of early Greek inscriptions; the other categories of early public inscriptions are lists of names of kings or athletic victors recorded for historical purposes, decrees, treaties, and records of public works, none of which is older than the sixth century. The oldest surviving inscription of a treaty is probably from 550–525 (Meiggs-Lewis 1969, no. 10). There may be genuine elements of a seventh-century foundation document for Cyrene in a preserved fourth-century inscription (ibid., no. 5), but we do not know if, or in what form, this document may have been originally inscribed.

By "public inscription" I refer not just to the inscription of material in a place where anyone may see it. Even private inscriptions, such as graffiti, may be inscribed in a public place. The significant point is that public inscriptions are inscribed by a public authority for public use. The early *thesmothetai* in Athens wrote down certain rules,[30] but although they probably inscribed these rules in a public place,[31] they did so, according to Aristotle, "for their own use." These rules would thus have had a fundamentally different purpose from that of Draco's laws. The *thesmothetai* probably derived these rules from decisions in cases in which they had been the judges, and we might note that in some Greek cities judicial scribes were called *mnēmones* ("rememberers") or *hieromnēmones* ("sacred rememberers"). According to Aristotle these officials recorded the decisions of the courts,[32] and their titles may reflect a period when certain judicial officials were charged with remembering previous decisions as a service for judges. With the advent of writing it would have been an easy step to preserve these decisions in writing.

The step from remembering previous decisions to writing them down, however, does not fundamentally alter the private nature of these written texts. Iceland provides an interesting illustration of this: in early times a "lawspeaker" apparently memorized a body of rules and recited them once a year.[33] After these "laws" were first written down (ca. A.D. 1118), numerous copies were made and kept by individuals for their own use. Soon these copies began to show many significant variations, and for several centuries there was no single authoritative copy. Courts had to decide between the different provisions of these private books, and although regulations were drawn up giving priority to certain of these law books, considerable confusion still existed.[34] The Icelandic experience shows that the mere recording of legal rules does not give them the status or authority of publicly inscribed laws.

30. Aristotle, *Ath. Pol.* 3.4; see chap. 3 above.

31. See p. 51, n. 2, above.

32. *Pol.* 1321B34–40; see Newman's note, ad loc., and cf. *IC* 4.42.B.6 and 4.72.9.32 with Willetts's note, ad loc. The fact that *mnēmones* are found in many Greek cities during classical times and later is no evidence for a system of oral preservation of law codes at an earlier time. In virtually all cases they are relatively minor officials.

33. See p. 10 above.

34. Jóhannesson 1974, 89–93; Hastrup 1985, 219–20.

The crucial step in the emergence of Greek law was not the writing down of judicial decisions or of general rules enunciated at trials, but rather the official publication of a law or set of laws. When the Locrians authorized Zaleucus to publish his laws, or when the city of Dreros authorized the inscription of a law representing what "was pleasing to the polis," at this point we may truly say that these cities were publicly inscribing laws. It is evident, moreover, that the public inscription of a law or set of laws presumes an act of legislation, a point we shall return to shortly.

With regard to publication, however, we should first note that the addition of a full set of signs for vowels made the Greek alphabet less ambiguous and thus easier to read than its Near-Eastern ancestors.[35] By the time of the earliest legal inscriptions literacy may have been fairly widely established in Greece, by which I mean that many people could manage to read a written text, although many others could not and the primary medium of communication was still oral. The nature of the Greek alphabet thus allowed the Greek laws to be more truly public documents than the Near-Eastern codes, about which Finkelstein has written:

> It is probably well to stress first of all that the *purpose* of the Lower Mesopotamian "law codes" was decidedly *not legislative*, if indeed it is not altogether anachronistic to speak of "legislation" in the ancient Mesopotamian context. These "law codes" . . . must be viewed in the first instance as royal apologia and testaments. Their primary purpose was to lay before the public, posterity, future kings, and, above all, the gods, evidence of the king's execution of his divinely ordained mandate.[36]

In other words, the Near-Eastern laws were not available for use by the people (or at least such was not the reason for their being in-

35. The fullest study of the special characteristics of the Greek alphabet is by Havelock 1982, 60–88 (originally published in *The Origins of Western Literacy.* Toronto 1976). Although he may go too far in claiming that the Greek alphabet "democratized literacy, or rather made democratization possible" (83), it seems clear that the Greek modifications made writing more accessible to the general public. The most recent survey of the evidence for Greek literacy is Burns, with references to earlier studies. He concludes that "from the end of the sixth century B.C. the vast majority of Athenian citizens were literate" (1981, 371).

36. Finkelstein 1961, 103; cf. Paul 1970, 23–26, Jackson 1975, 26–29, Whitelam 1979, 17–37.

scribed) but rather were intended to inspire greater respect for the monarch.[37]

In contrast, the early Greek codes were true legislation, embodying the fundamental notion that the actual rules, both substantive and procedural, governing the operation of a community's judicial system should be made publicly available for all to read and to employ in a legal action, or indeed in their everyday lives. To be sure, the ordinary Greek might need help with fine points of the law, and "interpreters" of the law existed in Athens,[38] but citizens could and generally were expected to handle their own legal affairs, and all citizens could and many did engage in jury duty. The archaic Greek polis, though by no means democratic (with rare exceptions), nonetheless considered its legal system and its laws to be public business, open to all citizens. The public nature of Greek laws has no parallel in the law codes of the Near East.

Another aspect of this fundamental difference between Greek laws and those of the Near East is that, even though the early Greeks often attributed their laws to a god or gods,[39] and even though much early Greek legislation was the work of individual lawgivers, their laws were in the first place authorized and sanctioned by the polis.[40] Indeed, the earliest surviving law from Dreros

37. The various Hebrew codes of law preserved in the Old Testament are different. They cover many different areas of human behavior, and some of the rules can scarcely be considered legal. As Paul says:

> Man's civil, moral and religious obligations all ultimately stem from God, and hence are interwoven within a single corpus of divinely given law. These three realms, which in extra-biblical societies would be incorporated respectively in law collections, wisdom literature, and priestly handbooks, are here combined into one body of prescriptions. (1970, 37)

38. One case in which these interpreters were consulted is described in Demosthenes 47.68–73.

39. In addition to the story that Zaleucus and others learned their laws from a god, note the Cretan practice of writing "Gods" at the beginning of several of their legal inscriptions (such as *IC* 4.72).

40. Cf. Lloyd 1979, 247–48, who discusses differences between Near-Eastern and Greek laws in terms of the higher personal sanction of a god or monarch found in Near-Eastern but not in most Greek codes. Wolff (1980), on the other hand, sees the ascription of some of the earliest Greek.law codes to gods as fundamental to Greek law and relates this to the Homeric idea that Zeus gave kings the scepter and *themistes*. In either case, however, the ascription of divine origin indicates only the importance of laws and legal procedure for the Greeks (see p. 24, n. 16, above). I see no support for the idea that they received either individual legal decisions or individual laws from the gods.

begins with the explicit statement that it has been enacted by the polis. The lawgivers, most of whom were not from the ruling elite, were, as far as we can tell, appointed in some manner by the polis for the purpose of enacting legislation, and the resulting laws were the property (so to speak) of the polis, authorized by it and sanctioned by its authority. In contrast, the Near-Eastern laws were authorized and sanctioned by a monarch or a small priestly class.[41]

We might recall in this regard the ending of Herodotus's story of the Mede Deioces.[42] Before he became king, Deioces judged cases publicly and openly in a system similar to that of preliterate Greece. After becoming king, however, his administration of justice changed; he judged cases privately after they were submitted in writing (presumably by specially trained scribes), and he sent out agents to insure that people were punished for their misdeeds. Herodotus is almost certainly contrasting the legal procedure of the contemporary Persians with that of the Greeks, and the story suggests the same special feature of the Greek system, open and public as opposed to closed and autocratically controlled, that we have noted with regard to the public inscription of their laws. The earliest Greek legislation, like early legal procedure, was a public phenomenon; as such it was quite different from any of its Near-Eastern predecessors.

This difference between Greek and Near-Eastern laws is clearly related to basic features of both cultures. Even under single rulers, such as the Homeric monarchs or the archaic tyrants, Greek cities were not subjected to the same sort of absolute authority characteristic of Near-Eastern kingdoms. Councils of other nobles advising or supporting a ruler are common in Homer,[43] and in the archaic period it appears that the tyrants could only acquire or retain their power with the support of at least a large minority of the people. In many cases the tyrants were in fact quite popular.

Given the more public nature of their society, it may have been no accident that when the Greeks adapted a Semitic script for their own use, they modified it in such a way that the new script could be

41. This is true of the Hebrew codes as well. It is also the case that many of the earliest written codes in England and on the Continent were the work of either a monarch or the church.

42. Herodotus 1.96–100; see chap. 2 above.

43. See Geddes 1984, 31–32. In addition to the positive evidence for assemblies, we might note that a characteristic of the uncivilized Cyclopes is that they have no assemblies (*Od.* 9.112).

more easily read than the Semitic model and would therefore be available to everyone. The development of a true alphabetic script precluded the sort of closed, scribal culture found in the Near East and also in Mycenean Greece of the Bronze Age.

Our task now is no longer to ask simply why the Greeks wrote down laws at this particular time but rather why they initiated the public inscription of laws and the acts of legislation necessary for public inscription. Why did so many cities appoint special lawgivers, sometimes even calling on an outsider for the task? In many cases the initial act of legislation was a special event, remembered for centuries as a significant point in the city's history. What forces were working in the seventh and sixth centuries to produce such large-scale and widespread legislative activity?

After the collapse of Mycenean culture around 1200 B.C. a significant change seems to have occurred in the organization of Greek society. The transition from the large Mycenean kingdom to the smaller, independent polis began not long after 1200,[44] though the polis did not reach its fully developed form until the archaic period. Specific conditions may have varied to some extent from city to city, but one development is evident everywhere, namely the increasing power of the polis. In his great work on the "solidarity of the family" Gustav Glotz long ago examined the general breakdown of the traditional control exercised by the head of the *oikos* ("household," or "extended family") over its other members, which took place during the archaic period, and the growth of the polis that accompanied it.[45] By 750 B.C. the polis was growing rapidly, and with the increase in material prosperity and the growth of the population everywhere in Greece from the eighth through the sixth centuries,[46] there was, perhaps inevitably, a trend toward greater regulation by the polis of the lives of its inhabitants.

In particular, as the city grew, opportunities for conflict must have increased, and it would become increasingly necessary that these conflicts be resolved and that procedures for settling disputes by peaceful means function well. As we have seen, public judicial procedures had already been established by the end of the eighth

44. For a good survey of Greece during the post-Mycenean "dark age," see Snodgrass 1971, 360–442.

45. Glotz 1904; cf. Gerner 1950. Although some of the details of Glotz's picture of early Greece have been altered, his basic thesis still remains valid.

46. See, most recently, Snodgrass 1980.

century; indeed it is possible that the establishment of formal judicial procedures went hand in hand with the establishment of the polis itself. But as the polis grew, the traditional voluntary procedure was apparently subject to increasing abuse by both judges and litigants and was proving inadequate. One of the important steps taken by the early polis was thus to strengthen and refine the judicial process and to reduce the scope of and bring under control the traditional means of self-help, which had long been the province of the family. This was no easy task, however, and during this period many cities seem to have experienced severe internal conflicts.

In response to this turmoil many cities turned to the relatively new technology of writing, which though known to the Greeks for about a century appears not to have been used for public inscriptions before the first laws were inscribed around the middle of the seventh century. It is possible that the recording of judicial decisions (see above) may have added some stability to the judicial process and may have inspired the idea that the public inscription of a set of laws would help reduce or eliminate some of the problems in the system. It is even possible (though I consider it unlikely) that the idea of inscribing a set of laws came from the Near East.

In order to write down a set of laws, however, one must first have a clearly recognizable body of rules, and as we have seen, the Greeks at this point did not.[47] It is easy from a modern perspective to say that "inscribed tablets were seen to be a better depositary of law, and a better security for its accurate preservation, than the memory of a number of persons,"[48] but such a view presumes the existence of a differentiated body of laws that simply did not exist until it was created by acts of legislation. The recording of judicial decisions may have provided a beginning, but the Greek cities must soon have realized that true legislation (often based, to be sure, on traditional customs) was needed before a set of laws could be publicly inscribed.

The decision to write down a set of laws was thus in effect a decision to enact legislation. It is hard to say which of these ideas may have been uppermost in the lawgivers' minds; indeed it is perhaps impossible to separate the two. The public inscription of laws presupposes an act of legislation, and the enactment of legislation pre-

47. One might compare the difficulty encountered by a modern colonial administrator trying to establish a written code by which to judge disputes among the native people. See, for example, Howell 1954, esp. 1–5.

48. Maine 1861, 9.

supposes the existence of a means of recognizing this special set of rules and granting it its special authority, which was clearly accomplished by public inscription.

It is evident that the task of legislation was beyond the ability of existing magistrates or political bodies, since most cities called upon a political outsider, sometimes even a foreigner, to provide them with a set of laws. In view of the apparently widespread feeling that the judicial process was in need of reform, it is not surprising that judicial magistrates were not entrusted with the task of drawing up new legislation. It is perhaps more difficult to explain, however, why (with few exceptions) the current rulers or the existing political bodies did not undertake the task, though we should remember that in some cases the same magistrates were charged with both political and judicial duties.[49] We can speculate that in the midst of political turmoil the appointment of a lawgiver was an act of negotiation and compromise—the result of a long period of struggle in which all factions in the city came to understand that if a law code was to have public authority, it could not be enacted by a single group. Indeed, the public appointment of a lawgiver may sometimes have resembled the traditional Greek process of voluntary submission of a private dispute to a mutually acceptable judge, since the lawgiver would have been appointed with the consent of most, if not all, of the feuding parties.

As usual, our best evidence is from Athens. Although the details of Draco's appointment as lawgiver are not known, it is generally accepted that the turmoil resulting from Cylon's failed attempt at tyranny, perhaps a decade earlier, provided at least part of the motivation.[50] Stroud suggests that the Alcmeonids and their non-aristocratic supporters may have arranged Draco's appointment. But if, as seems likely, in the decade following the conspiracy both factions had suffered losses from the continual feuding, then the Cylonians may have been as ready as their opponents to agree on a lawgiver for the city.

Better evidence exists for Solon's appointment. He himself tells

49. The *kosmoi* in Cretan cities certainly had both political and judicial functions, and Hesiod's kings probably had some political as well as judicial power.

50. See Gagarin 1981a, 20–21; Stroud 1968, 70–74. Cf. Andrewes: "Popular discontent may have played a part in promoting the change [sc. the publication of Draco's law]. But strife within the governing class had shown itself as a danger in the recent affair of the Cylonians, and that may well have weighed more" (1982, 370).

us that he favored neither the common people nor the rich and powerful, but "stood holding a strong shield in front of each side and allowed neither to triumph unfairly."[51] Solon saw himself as a mediator, and we may assume that his appointment had at least the tacit approval of both sides. And though the evidence for other Greek cities is slim, it suggests that the Athenian pattern was repeated elsewhere. Even in Mytilene, Pittacus was apparently appointed tyrant by the people after a long period of bitter feuding among aristocratic factions.

The Cretan cities seem to have followed a somewhat different path, inscribing laws singly at first and then amending and reinscribing them in groups at a later date.[52] We can only speculate about the reasons for this special feature of Cretan laws, since we know very little of the history of any Cretan city during this period. The archaeological evidence, however, reveals a relatively prosperous, artistically advanced culture, and it is possible that Cretan cities somehow avoided the turmoil so common elsewhere. They may thus have felt no need for a special lawgiver or a special set of laws, but rather the existing political bodies simply enacted laws as they were needed.

It is clear that even the earliest inscribed laws in Crete were newly enacted and did not just record an established rule. The law from Dreros, for example, was explicitly enacted by the polis and almost certainly contained a new regulation, though it may have been based on traditional practice.[53] It is unlikely, moreover, that this law limiting the term of a *kosmos* could be the written record of an earlier judicial decision, since a *kosmos* would be unlikely to impose such restrictions on himself and his colleagues. Similarly, the early law from Gortyn requiring a *kosmos* to pay a fine himself if it is not

51. Solon frag. 5.5–6; cf. frags. 36–37 (24–25D).

52. Our evidence is most plentiful for Gortyn. One of the earliest inscriptions, *IC* 4.1 from the early sixth century, apparently contains five separately inscribed laws in five different hands. Later inscriptions (e.g., *IC* 4.41) contain groups of laws on various topics; some of these, like the laws on the Great Code (*IC* 4.72; see Gagarin 1983), probably were earlier inscribed elsewhere. The new sixth-century inscription from Phaestus (*SEG* 32.908; see p. 93, n. 42, above) provides the first possible evidence for large-scale inscription of laws at that city. The small extant fragment may have formed part of a larger wall.

53. A three-year term may have been traditional for a *kosmos*, but it is unlikely that this law would have been enacted if this limit had not been exceeded by some *kosmoi*.

paid by the person who was assessed it is hardly likely to have resulted from the recording of a judicial decision in which a *kosmos* held himself liable for an unpaid fine. Thus although the Cretan cities preferred continual small-scale enactments to the large-scale legislation of most other Greek cities, in both cases there was a need for enactment by the polis or its authorized agent before any laws could be publicly inscribed.

The new laws, as we have seen, concerned both legal procedure and those areas of conflict most likely to be subject to legal procedure (torts and family law). Some laws focused directly on the judicial process, such as the Chian and Eretrian laws preserved in inscriptions. Others, such as Draco's homicide law, regulated legal procedure with respect to a particular substantive law. In either case the mere fact of public inscription would have given the new laws an authority hitherto unattainable and must therefore have increased the pressure on families and individuals to use the judicial institutions of the polis in settling their disputes rather than resorting to self-help. We have also seen that the greater amount of detail that could be included in written laws made possible for the first time a truly compulsory judicial procedure.

This was clearly the purpose of the set of laws at the beginning of the Great Code at Gortyn forbidding the seizure of a person before a trial (i.e., by self-help). Even a law like the homicide law from Cumae, which determined the guilt of some killers on the basis of a specific number of witnesses presented by the victim's family, has the effect of strengthening the control of the polis over the treatment of homicide cases, since the parties must now settle their case according to the specific rule of the polis, even if they do so on their own without using the public legal institutions.

The substantive legislation of early Greece also strengthened the control of the polis. Even though many of the new tort laws (probably including Draco's homicide law) may have simply affirmed the traditional penalties for wrongs, by giving these penalties an official authority the polis would help regularize judicial proceedings and reduce to some extent the flexibility of individuals in disputes. Family laws, for which we have evidence at Gortyn from an early period[54] as well as from Athens and a few other cities, also led to

---

54. See, e.g., *IC* 4.17, 20, 21; most of the fifth-century Great Code (*IC* 4.72) concerns family law and it is likely that many of its provisions were initially enacted in the archaic period.

greater control by the polis over the affairs of families. True, Solon's laws limiting the power of the head of the family to sell his children or requiring the support of one's parents or allowing for adoption were probably intended not to weaken families but to help them survive, yet the need for such laws probably indicates the precarious condition of many families at the time. Overall, the enactment of such laws eventually led to even greater involvement of the polis in the affairs of the family. For example, the law allowing a man without direct heirs to adopt a son was presumably intended to help preserve the family and its property intact, but it also opened up a large area for litigation and led to innumerable suits that in the end had to be decided by the judicial apparatus of the polis.

Finally, the public laws of Solon also led clearly to greater control by the polis over the lives of its inhabitants. Economic activity was controlled, at least in certain areas, and the idea that political service to the city was everyone's obligation was beginning to take hold. Even laws regulating private matters, moreover, could implicitly convey the notion that members of a community had ipso facto certain rights and obligations under the law. Draco's homicide law, for example, treats the killing of a properly exiled killer just like the killing of an Athenian, implying that any "Athenian" has certain rights by law. The concept of "citizenship" undoubtedly evolved considerably in the period from Draco to Aristotle,[55] but already in this provision we can see the basic idea that certain people belong to a particular polis. In this and other ways the early written legislation of the Greeks must have strengthened the sense that a person's identity was in large part determined by membership in a specific political community, with the result that by Aristotle's time it was virtually a truism that "man is by nature an animal of the polis" (zōon politikon).[56]

The enactment of written legislation thus established without doubt the authority of the polis over its inhabitants. Not that written legislation was the only means of doing this; Sparta appears consciously to have rejected the use of written laws and to have relied on an increasing degree of control over the educational system to achieve a similarly strong authority over its citizens. Most other cit-

55. See Manville 1980.
56. Aristotle, *Pol.* 1253A2–3.

ies, however, turned to the new technology of writing for the means to control a growing and increasingly contentious population.

The public inscription of the early law codes would not necessarily strengthen the supporters of one particular form of government, democratic, aristocratic, oligarchic, or tyrannical, but rather, by reducing the feuding among members of the ruling class and by increasing the reach and the efficiency of the judicial system, it would probably support whatever group happened to be ruling in the city at the time. In some cities, as in the case of Athens, publication of laws might support democratic elements in the city and eventually lead to greater democracy, but in others written laws might support a tyrant (Pittacus in Mytilene) or an aristocratic government (in Locri, Catana, and elsewhere). Of course others in the polis benefitted as well, and to the extent that the judicial process functioned more fairly and efficiently, all citizens were better off.

In sum, whatever the particular form of government, all Greek cities during the archaic period were gradually increasing their power at the expense of that of individual families; and as the size and complexity of the polis increased, almost all cities saw the need for an official set of written laws, publicly displayed, to confirm the authority of the polis in bringing order to the lives of its citizens. Written laws thus served the interest not of any single group or political party but of all the citizens as incorporated in that unique institution, the polis.

7

CONCLUSION

We have seen that the emergence of law in Greece during the archaic period took place in two distinct stages. First in the preliterate period the basic elements of judicial procedure were established, providing a formal means for the public settlement of disputes by recognized third parties. This procedure depended ultimately on the voluntary submission of disputes by both litigants, although it appears that by the end of the eighth century many, if not most, Greeks felt strong public pressure to submit their disputes to this legal process rather than use force, as under the older system of self-help. High-ranking members of society may have resisted this pressure more often than others. Enforcement of judicially obtained settlements was problematic, and resort to self-help may have been more common for this purpose than for obtaining a settlement in the first place. But whatever its limitations, Homer and Hesiod place a high value on judicial procedure as a vital element in the life of a peaceful community, the standard form of which is the polis.[1]

During the eighth and seventh centuries the population of most Greek cities grew rapidly, as did the level of economic activity. Although the polis was equipped with only rudimentary political institutions, these were steadily gaining power as the traditional solidarity of the family was eroded. Except in Crete few large cities escaped the troubles of internal dissension; in some, strife was almost continual. It is apparent that the judicial system, perhaps because of these trends, came under increasing criticism. Pressure for reform was widespread, both in order to reduce the corruption of the magistrates and to improve the efficiency and fairness of the process.

In about the middle of the eighth century came the discovery of alphabetic writing. Although at first apparently limited to private inscriptions, the use of writing spread rapidly through the Greek

1. See Luce 1978.

world and eventually became the key element in the development of a true legal system. Writing may first have been used for the recording of settlements or of general rules governing settlements in individual cases. Previously these had sometimes been remembered, perhaps by specially trained officials, but now they could be recorded to provide guidance in future cases.

The most important use of the new technology, however, was the public inscription of those rules that were to apply in judicial settlements, a step that also required a public act of legislation. The movement to enact legislation swept over Greece from about the middle of the seventh to the middle of the sixth centuries. The importance of this undertaking was not that it made available to the public rules that had hitherto been kept from it, since before the public inscription of laws there did not exist any recognized body of rules for use in the judicial process. Rather, the desire for publicly inscribed rules forced the political authorities to decide precisely which rules they were going to inscribe and in what form. In other words, the availability of writing led the Greeks to the crucial step of differentiating from the mass of their stated and unstated norms, including customs, traditions, maxims, fables, proverbs and previous judicial decisions, a body of rules specifically to be used in the judicial settlement of disputes. It mattered not whether this legislation was the product of a single legislator or of an anonymous body, or whether laws were enacted singly or in a set. What mattered was that the act of legislation, essential to the existence of a true legal system, had been invented. Henceforth, the laws of a polis would be a separate, recognizable body of norms, differentiated from all the other rules of the society.

It is legitimate to speak of the "invention" of legislation in Greece, since even if we grant the status of legislation to the Near-Eastern law codes, Greek legislation was a significantly different activity, the public action of a political community, the polis, rather than the private action of an individual. The laws of Hammurabi, like those of the other Near-Eastern monarchs, were proclaimed (we can hardly say enacted) and published to serve his own ends; those of Zaleucus, Draco, and the rest were enacted specifically at the request of the polis to serve the needs of its citizens. Thus from its beginning Greek law exemplifies the fundamentally public character of Greek culture, of which Athenian democracy was just the most extreme manifestation.

In a recent work on the origins of Greek science[2] Geoffrey Lloyd has suggested that certain distinctive features of the Greek polis may have played a significant role in the development of scientific thought. In particular he argues that the open and competitive nature of political and legal institutions (in contrast with those of the Near East) contributed to the formation of notions of evidence, argument and proof. Most of Lloyd's evidence for the nature of Greek political life are drawn from democratic Athens; he says relatively little about law either outside of Athens or before Solon, although he claims that the distinctive features of this life were also present in other, nondemocratic cities.

Lloyd's argument is a strong one, but it can be extended and, I think, strengthened if we consider a broader range of material. The evidence we have examined for law, and especially for legal procedure,[3] throughout Greece from the time of Homer indicates clearly that those distinctive features of the Greek polis noted by Lloyd both existed earlier and were more widespread than he allows.[4] The legal and political reforms of Solon, though significant in this regard, are only one small part of the total development of Greek law.

In general, the public inscription of laws did not result in large changes in the substance of rules of conduct. The most significant changes were procedural, and perhaps the most significant of these was the final step in the long transition from voluntary to compulsory procedure, brought about by a precision of details not found before the introduction of written laws. Otherwise, the procedural innovations of the archaic period seem intended to improve rather than change the existing system by reducing the possibility of corruption, facilitating access to the legal process, and assisting in the enforcement of settlements.

Although classical Greek and particularly Athenian law is often criticized for its lack of systematization and the absence of profes-

2. Lloyd 1979, 246–64.

3. Lloyd does not mention the Greek emphasis on procedure, though it is notable that the legal metaphors we find in early Greek thought, which are important for Lloyd (see 247–48), are primarily drawn from procedural justice.

4. Cf. Lloyd-Jones: "While I agree with Lloyd that the legal and political conditions of Greek life were such as to conduce to the prevalence of the notions of argument and proof, I would place the origins of that prevalence a great deal earlier than he does, certainly long before the time of Homer" (1983, 183). Lloyd-Jones also cites the distinctive nature of Greek religion as an important factor in this intellectual development.

sional jurists, for the Greeks themselves law was one of the notable achievements of their culture. We may recall the words of Hesiod with which we began this study: "Zeus established the following way of life for men: whereas for fish and beasts and winged birds it is the custom to eat one another, since there is no law among them, to men he gave law, which is by far the best thing." Hesiod is thinking, of course, of judicial procedure, and our study has shown that even after the Greeks began to write laws, they focused their attention primarily on procedural law. And the main trend in procedural law was to make the system open to, as well as controlled by, the people.

We have thus seen that the fundamental characteristics of classical Greek law, in particular the public enactment of laws and the heavy emphasis on legal procedure, were essentially the creation of the archaic age. The introduction of writing at the beginning of this period, especially in the modified script created by the Greeks, was certainly a prerequisite for these legal developments, but the more important factors were perhaps political. The highly authoritarian types of government common to the rest of the world at the time were unsuitable for the relatively small Greek polis, which was thus developing its own, less centralized form of government. One purpose of this book has been to show that among the most important creations of this unique political entity, the polis, was the rule of law, and that although laws and legal procedures were known in various forms in other parts of the world, the Greeks created something different. For the first time the law was made available to and was intended to be used by the entire citizenry. In most other "advanced" cultures law came to be controlled by a relatively small group of lawyers or jurists, often rather removed from the majority of citizens. Throughout their independent existence, however, the Greek cities held to their ideal of keeping the law in the hands of all citizens. The system may have had its drawbacks in practice, but the ideal is a worthy one and we would do well to remember it.

BIBLIOGRAPHY

Greek authors are cited from the standard editions; all are available in English translation in the Loeb Classical Library series (Harvard University Press). Note that I cite Plutarch according to the chapter and section numbers of the Teubner text (*Vitae Parallelae*. K. Ziegler, ed. Leipzig 1960–); in some cases the section numbers in the Loeb translations differ slightly from these. Editions with commentary are cited by the name of the modern commentator and full references are given below.

Note: *Ath. Pol.* = Aristotle (?), *Athēnaiōn Politeia* (*The Constitution of Athens*).

ABBREVIATIONS

AJP   *American Journal of Philology.*
BCH   *Bulletin de correspondance hellénique.*
BSA   *Annual of the British School at Athens.*
CAH   *Cambridge Ancient History.*
CP   *Classical Philology.*
CQ   *Classical Quarterly.*
FGH   Jacoby, ed. *Die Fragmente der griechischen Historiker.*
FHG   Müller, ed. *Fragmenta Historicorum Graecorum.*
GRBS *Greek, Roman, and Byzantine Studies.*
HSCP *Harvard Studies in Classical Philology.*
IC   Guarducci, ed. *Inscriptiones Creticae.*
IG   *Inscriptiones Graecae.*
JHS   *Journal of Hellenic Studies.*
RE   A. Pauly, G. Wissowa, and W. Kroll, *Real-Encyclopädie der classischen Altertumswissenschaft.*
RIDA *Revue internationale des droits de l'antiquité.*
SEG   *Supplementum Epigraphicum Graecum.*
TAPA *Transactions of the American Philological Association.*
ZPE   *Zeitschrift fur Papyrologie und Epigraphik.*
ZSS   *Zeitschrift der Savigny Stiftung,* Romanistische Abteilung.

Adcock, F. E. 1927. "Literary Tradition and Early Greek Code-Makers." *Cambridge Historical Journal* 2: 95–109.
Adkins, Arthur W. H. 1960. *Merit and Responsibility.* Oxford.
———. 1982. "Values, Goals, and Emotions in the *Iliad.*" CP 77: 292–326.

Anderson, Ovind. 1976. "Some Thoughts on the Shield of Achilles." *Symbolae Osloenses* 51: 5–18.

Andrewes, A. 1982. "The Growth of the Athenian State" and "The Tyranny of Peisistratus." In *CAH*. 2nd ed. 3.3: 360–416. Cambridge.

Armstrong, A. MacC. 1950. "Trial by Combat among the Greeks." *Greece and Rome* 19: 73–79.

Asheri, David. 1963. "Laws of Inheritance, Distribution of Land and Political Constitutions in Ancient Greece." *Historia* 12: 1–21.

Beattie, Arthur J. 1975. "Some Notes on the Spensitheos Decree," *Kadmos* 14: 8–47.

Beloch, Karl Julius. 1912–1926. *Griechische Geschichte*. 2nd ed. Vol. 1, 2 parts. Berlin and Leipzig.

Benveniste, Emile. 1973. *Indo-European Language and Society*. Coral Gables, Fla. (Originally *Le vocabulaire des institutions Indo-Européennes*. Paris, 1969.)

Binchy, D. A. 1943. "The Linguistic and Historical Value of the Irish Law Tracts." *Proceedings of the British Academy* 29: 195–227.

Boardman, John. 1970. "Orientalen auf Kreta." In *Dädalische Kunst auf Kreta im 7. Jahrhundert v. Chr.* Hamburg.

Bohannan, Paul. 1957. *Justice and Judgment among the Tiv*. Oxford.

———. 1965. "The Differing Realms of the Law." In *The Ethnography of Law*, ed. Laura Nader (suppl. to *American Anthropologist* 67.2), 33–42. Reprinted in *Law and Warfare*, ed. P. Bohannan (Garden City, N. Y. 1967), 43–56.

Bonner, R. J., and G. Smith. 1930. *The Administration of Justice from Homer to Aristotle*. Vol. 1. Chicago.

Boring, Terrence A. 1979. *Literacy in Ancient Sparta. Mnemosyne* Supplement 54. Leiden.

Bryce, James. 1901. *Studies in History and Jurisprudence*. Vol. 1. New York.

Burkert, Walter. 1985. *Greek Religion*. Oxford. (Originally *Griechische Religion der archaischen und klassischen Epoche*. Stuttgart 1977.)

Burns, Alfred. 1981. "Athenian Literacy in the Fifth Century B.C." *Journal of the History of Ideas* 42: 371–87.

Bury, J. B., and Russell Meiggs. 1975. *A History of Greece*. 4th ed. London.

Cairns, Francis. 1984. "*Chremata dokima: IG* XII,9,1273 and 1274 and the Early Coinage of Eretria." *ZPE* 54: 145–55.

Calhoun, George M. 1927. *The Growth of Criminal Law in Ancient Greece*. Berkeley and Los Angeles.

———. 1944. *Introduction to Greek Legal Science*. Oxford.

———. 1962. "Polity and Society: The Homeric Picture." In *A Companion to Homer*, ed. A. J. B. Wace and Frank H. Stubbings, 431–52. London. (originally written ca. 1940).

Cantarella, Eva. 1979. *Norma e Sanzione in Omero*. Milan.

Cartledge, Paul. 1978. "Literacy in the Spartan Oligarchy." *JHS* 98: 25–37.

Cerri, Giovanni. 1979. *Legislazione orale e tragedia greca.* Naples.

Coldstream, J. N. 1977. *Geometric Greece.* New York.

Comaroff, John L., and Simon Roberts. 1981. *Rules and Processes: The Cultural Logic of Dispute in an African Context.* Chicago.

Cook, W. W. 1933. "'Substance' and 'Procedure' in the Conflict of Laws." *Yale Law Journal* 42: 333–58.

David, Ephraim. 1984. "Solon, Neutrality and Partisan Literature of Late Fifth-Century Athens." *Museum Helveticum* 41: 129–38.

Demargne, P., and H. van Effenterre. 1937. "Recherches à Dréros." *BCH* 61: 333–48.

Diamant, Steven. 1982. "Theseus and the Unification of Attica." *Hesperia* Supplement 19: 38–47.

Diamond, A. S. 1971. *Primitive Law Past and Present.* London.

Di Vita, A., and E. Cantarella. 1982. "Inscrizione arcaica giuridica da Festòs." *Annuario della Scuola Archeologica di Atene* 56 [1978]: 429–35.

Drewes, Robert. 1983. *Basileus: The Evidence for Kingship in Geometric Greece.* New Haven.

Driver, G. R., and John C. Miles. 1952. *The Babylonian Laws.* Oxford.

Dunbabin, T. J. 1948. *The Western Greeks.* Oxford.

Dworkin, Ronald. 1977. *Taking Rights Seriously.* Cambridge, Mass.

Edwards, G. P., and R. B. Edwards. 1977. "The Meaning and Etymology of *poinakistes.*" *Kadmos* 16: 131–40.

Ehrenberg, Victor. 1943. "An Early Source of Polis-Constitution." *CQ* 37: 14–18.

England, E. B. 1921. *The Laws of Plato.* 2 Vols. Manchester.

Evans-Pritchard, E. E. 1940. *The Nuer.* Oxford.

Finkelstein, J. J. 1961. "Ammisaduqa's Edict and the Babylonian 'Law Codes'." *Journal of Cuneiform Studies* 15: 91–104.

Finley, M. I. 1978. *The World of Odysseus.* 2nd ed. New York.

Fitzgerald, Robert, trans. 1974. Homer, *The Iliad.* Garden City, N. Y.

Foote, Peter. 1977. "Oral and Literary Tradition in Early Scandinavian Law: Aspects of a Problem." In *Oral Tradition, Literary Tradition,* ed. Hans Bekker-Nielsen et al., 47–55. Odense.

Forrest, W. G. 1960. "The Tribal Organization of Chios." *BSA* 55: 172–89.

———. 1963. "The Date of the Lykourgan Reforms in Sparta." *Phoenix* 17: 157–79.

———. 1966. *The Emergence of Greek Democracy.* London.

Frank, Jerome. 1930. *Law and the Modern Mind.* New York.

Freeman, Edward A. 1892. *The History of Sicily.* Vol. 3. Oxford.

Gagarin, Michael. 1973. "*Dikē* in the *Works and Days.*" *CP* 68: 81–94.

———. 1974. "Hesiod's Dispute with Perses." *TAPA* 104: 103–11.

———. 1976. *Aeschylean Drama.* Berkeley and Los Angeles.

————. 1979. "The Prosecution of Homicide in Athens." *GRBS* 20: 301–23.

————. 1981a. *Drakon and Early Athenian Homicide Law.* New Haven.

————. 1981b. "The Thesmothetai and the Earliest Athenian Tyranny Law." *TAPA* 111: 71–77.

————. 1982. "The Organization of the Gortyn Law Code." *GRBS* 23: 129–46.

————. 1983. "Antilochus' Strategy: The Chariot Race in *Iliad* 23." *CP* 78: 35–39.

Gallavotti, Carlo. 1977. "Scritture della Sicilia ed altre epigrafi arcaiche." *Helikon* 17: 97–136.

Geddes, A. G. 1984. "Who's Who in 'Homeric' Society?" *CQ* 34: 17–36.

Gerner, Erich. 1950. "Historisch-soziologische Entwicklungstendenzen im attischen Recht." *ZSS* 67: 1–46.

Gernet, Louis. 1955. *Droit et société dans la Grèce ancienne.* Paris.

————. 1968. *Anthropologie de la Grèce antique.* Paris. (Eng. trans. Baltimore 1981.)

Gilbert, Gustav. 1897. "Beiträge zur Entwickelungsgeschichte des griechischen Gerichtsverfahrens und des griechischen Rechtes." *Jahrbücher für classische Philologie,* Supplementband 23: 443–536.

Gjerset, Knut. 1924. *History of Iceland.* New York.

Glotz, Gustave. 1904. *La solidarité de la famille dans le droit criminel en Grèce.* Paris.

Gluckman, Max. 1955. *The Judicial Process among the Barotse of Northern Rhodesia.* Manchester.

————. 1965a. *The Ideas in Barotse Jurisprudence.* New Haven.

————. 1965b. *Politics, Law and Ritual in Tribal Society.* London.

————. 1974. "African Traditional Law in Historical Perspective." *Proceedings of the British Academy* 60: 295–337.

Graham, A. J. 1982. "The Western Greeks." In *CAH.* 2nd ed. 3.3: 163–95. Cambridge.

Griffith, Mark. 1983. "Personality in Hesiod." *Classical Antiquity* 2: 37–65.

Guarducci, Margharita. 1935–50. *Inscriptiones Creticae.* 4 Vols. Rome.

Gulliver, P. H. 1963. *Social Control in an African Society.* London.

Hansen, Mogens Herman. 1975. *Eisangelia: The Sovereignty of the People's Court in Athens in the Fourth Century* B.C. *and the Impeachment of Generals and Politicians.* Odense.

————. 1976. *Apagoge, Endeixis and Ephegesis against Kakourgoi, Atimoi and Pheugontes.* Odense.

————. 1978. "*Nomos* and *Psēphisma* in Fourth-Century Athens." *GRBS* 19: 315–30.

————. 1980. "*Eisangelia* in Athens: A Reply." *JHS* 100: 89–95.

————. 1981. "The Prosecution of Homicide in Athens: A Reply." *GRBS* 22: 11–30.

————. 1981–82. "The Athenian *Heliaia* from Solon to Aristotle." *Classica et Mediaevalia* 33: 9–47.

Harrison A. R. W. 1968–71. *The Law of Athens*. Vol. 1: *The Family and Property*; Vol. 2: *Procedure*. Oxford.

Hart, H. L. A. 1961. *The Concept of Law*. Oxford.

————. 1967. "Philosophy of Law, Problems of." In *The Encyclopedia of Philosophy*, ed. Paul Edwards, 6: 264–76. New York.

————, ed. 1970. Jeremy Bentham, *Of Laws in General*. London.

————. 1983. *Essays in Jurisprudence and Philosophy*. Oxford.

Hastrup, Kirsten. 1985. *Culture and History in Medieval Iceland*. Oxford.

Havelock, Eric A. 1969. "*Dikaiosynē*: An Essay in Greek Intellectual History." *Phoenix* 23: 49–70.

————. 1978. *The Greek Concept of Justice*. Cambridge, Mass.

————. 1982. *The Literate Revolution in Greece and Its Cultural Consequences*. Princeton.

Headlam, J. W. 1892–93. "The Procedure of the Gortynian Inscription." *JHS* 13: 48–69.

Hignett, C. 1952. *A History of the Athenian Constitution*. Oxford.

Hoebel, E. Adamson. 1954. *The Law of Primitive Man*. Cambridge, Mass.

Hommel, Hildebrecht. 1969. "Die Gerichtsszene auf dem Schild des Achilleus." In *Politeia und Res Publica*, ed. Rudolf Starks. Palingenesia 6: 11–38. Wiesbaden.

Howell, P. P. 1954. *A Manual of Nuer Law*. Oxford.

Humphreys, S. C. 1978. *Anthropology and the Greeks*. London.

————. 1983. "The Evolution of Legal Process in Ancient Attica." In *Tria Corda: Scritti in onore di Arnaldo Momigliano*, 229–56. Como.

————. 1985a. "Law as Discourse." *History and Anthropology* 1: 241–64.

————. 1985b. "Social Relations on Stage: Witnesses in Classical Athens." *History and Anthropology* 1: 313–69.

Huxley, George. 1962. *Early Sparta*. Cambridge, Mass.

Isager, Signe, and M. H. Hansen. 1975. *Aspects of Athenian Society in the Fourth Century B.C.* Odense.

Jackson, Bernard S. 1975. *Essays in Jewish and Comparative Legal History*. Leiden.

Jacoby, Felix. 1923– . *Die Fragmente der griechischen Historiker*. Berlin and Leiden.

————. 1949. *Atthis*. Oxford.

Janko, Richard. 1982. *Homer, Hesiod and the Hymns: Diachronic Development in Epic Diction*. Cambridge.

Jeffery, L. H. 1956. "The Courts of Justice in Archaic Chios." *BSA* 51: 157–67.

———. 1961a. *The Local Scripts of Archaic Greece.* Oxford.

———. 1961b. "The Pact of the First Settlers at Cyrene." *Historia* 10: 139–47.

———. 1976. *Archaic Greece.* London.

———. 1982. "Greek Alphabetic Writing." In *CAH.* 2nd ed. 3.3: 819–33. Cambridge.

Jeffery, L. H., and A. Morpurgo-Davies. 1970. "*Poinikastas* and *poinika-zein*: BM 1969. 4–2.1, A New Archaic Inscription from Crete." *Kadmos* 9: 118–54.

Jensen, Minna Skafte. 1980. *The Homeric Question and the Oral-Formulaic Theory.* Copenhagen.

Jóhannesson, Jón. 1974. *A History of the Old Icelandic Commonwealth.* University of Manitoba Press. (Originally *Islendinga Saga.* Reykjavik 1956.)

Johnston, Alan. 1983. "The Extent and Use of Literacy: the Archaeological Evidence." In *The Greek Renaissance of the Eighth Century* B.C.: *Tradition and Innovation*, ed. Robin Hägg, 63–68. Stockholm.

Kakridis, J. T. 1975. "Mestra: zu Hesiods frg. 43a M.-W." *ZPE* 18: 17–25.

Kelsen, Hans. 1947. "The Metamorphoses of the Idea of Justice." In *Interpretations of Modern Legal Philosophies: Essays in Honor of R. Pound*, ed. Paul Sayre, 390–418. New York.

Kocourek, Albert, and John H. Wigmore. 1915. *Sources of Ancient and Primitive Law.* Boston.

Köhler, Ludwig. 1956. *Hebrew Man.* English trans. London. (German ed. 1953).

Latte, Kurt. 1920. *Heiliges Recht.* Tübingen.

———. 1946. "Der Rechtsgedanke im archaischen Griechentum." *Antike und Abendland* 2: 63–76.

Levy, E. 1978. "Notes sur la chronologie athénienne au VIe siècle." *Historia* 27: 513–21.

Linforth, I. M. 1919. *Solon the Athenian.* Berkeley and Los Angeles.

Lipsius, Justus Hermann. 1905–15. *Das attische Recht und Rechtsverfahren.* 3 Vols. Leipzig.

Llewellyn, Karl. 1951. *The Bramble Bush.* 2nd ed. New York.

Lloyd, G. E. R. 1979. *Magic, Reason and Experience: Studies in the Origins and Development of Greek Science.* Cambridge.

Lloyd-Jones, Hugh. 1983. *The Justice of Zeus.* 2nd ed. Berkeley.

Luce, J. V. 1978. "The *Polis* in Homer and Hesiod." *Proceedings of the Royal Irish Academy* 78: 1–15.

MacDowell, D. M. 1978. *The Law in Classical Athens.* London.

Maffi, Alberto. 1983. *Studi di epigrafia giuridica greca.* Milan.

Maine, Sir Henry. 1861. *Ancient Law.* London. (Citations from Everyman's Library Edition, London 1917).

Mair, Lucy. 1962. *Primitive Government.* Bloomington, Ind.

Malinowski, Bronislaw. 1926. *Crime and Custom in Savage Society.* London.

Mandel, Michael. 1979. "Dworkin, Hart, and the Problem of Theoretical Perspective." *Law and Society Review* 14: 57–82.

Manville, Brook. 1980. "Solon's Law of Stasis and *Atimia* in Archaic Athens." *TAPA* 110: 213–21.

McDonald, William A. 1956. "Note on a Fragment of an Archaic Inscription from Dreros." *Hesperia* 25: 69–72.

Meiggs, Russell, and David Lewis. 1969. *A Selection of Greek Historical Inscriptions.* Oxford.

Merkelbach, R. 1968. "Hesiod fr. 43(a)41ff. M.-W." *ZPE* 3: 134–35.

Merkelbach R., and M. L. West. 1967. *Fragmenta Hesiodea.* Oxford.

Mondi, Robert. 1980. "*Skēptouchoi basileis*: An Argument for Divine Kingship in Early Greece." *Arethusa* 13: 203–216.

Moore, S. F. 1978. *Law as Process.* London.

Mühl, Max. 1928. "Die Gesetze des Zaleukos und Charondas." *Klio* 22: 105–24, 432–63.

———. 1933. *Untersuchungen zur altorientalischen und althellenischen Gesetzgebung.* Klio Beiheft 29. Berlin.

Müller, K. 1841–70. *Fragmenta Historicorum Graecorum.* 5 Vols. Paris.

Nader, Laura, ed. 1969. *Law in Culture and Society.* Chicago.

Nader, Laura, and Harry F. Todd, Jr. 1978. *The Disputing Process—Law in Ten Societies.* New York.

Nance, John. 1975. *The Gentle Tasaday.* New York.

Newman, W. L. 1902. *The Politics of Aristotle.* Vols. 2–4. Oxford.

Oehler, J. 1922. "Kosmoi." *RE* 11: 1495–98.

Oliver, James H. 1959. "Text of the So-called Constitution of Chios from the First Half of the Sixth Century B.C." *AJP* 80: 296–301.

Ostwald, Martin. 1969. *Nomos and the Beginnings of Athenian Democracy.* Oxford.

———. 1973. "Was There a Concept *agraphos nomos* in Classical Greece?" *Phronesis* Suppl. 1: 70–104.

Page, Denys. 1955. *Sappho and Alcaeus.* Oxford.

Palmer, L. R. 1950. "The Indo-European Origins of Greek Justice." *Transactions of the Philological Society* (Oxford): 149–68.

Paoli, Ugo Enrico. 1949. "La loi de Solon sur les distances." *Revue historique du droit français et étranger* 27: 505–17. Reprinted in *Altri studi di diritto greco e romano* (Milan 1976) 571–83.

Parker, Robert. 1983. *Miasma: Pollution and Purification in Early Greek Religion.* Oxford.

Paul, Shalom M. 1970. *Studies in the Book of the Covenant in the Light of Cuneiform and Biblical Law.* Leiden.

Pfeiffer, Robert H. 1941. *Introduction to the Old Testament.* New York.

Piccirilli, Luigi. 1978. "La legge di Solone sulla dote (Plut., *Sol.* 20,6)." In

Scritti storico-epigrafici in memoria di Marcello Zambelli, ed. Lidio Gasperini (Univ. di Macerata, Pubbl. della fac. di lettere e filosofia 5), 321–24.

———. 1981. "'Nomoi' cantati e 'nomoi' scritti." *Civiltà classica e cristiana* 2: 7–14.

Pollock, Fredrick, and F. W. Maitland. 1898. *The History of English Law Before the Time of Edward I*. 2nd ed. Cambridge.

Pounder, Robert L. 1984. "The Origin of *theoi* in Inscription-Heading." In *Studies Presented to Sterling Dow on his Eightieth Birthday*, ed. W. T. Loomis et al. (*GRBS* Monograph 10, Durham, N.C.), 243–50.

Primmer, Adolf. 1970. "Homerische Gerichtsszenen." *Wiener Studien* 83: 5–13.

Pringsheim, F. 1957. "Some Causes of Codification." *RIDA* 4: 301–11.

Rabel, E. 1915. "*Dikē Exoulēs* und Verwandtes." *ZSS* 36: 340–90.

Radcliffe-Brown, A. R. 1933a. "Law, Primitive." In *Encyclopedia of the Social Sciences*. 9: 202–6. New York.

———. 1933b, "Sanction, Social." ibid., 12: 531–34.

Rawls, John. 1971. *A Theory of Justice*. Cambridge, Mass.

Reid, J. P. 1970. *A Law of Blood*. New York.

Rhodes, P. J. 1979. "*Eisangelia* in Athens." *JHS* 99: 103–14.

———. 1981. *A Commentary on the Aristotelian Athenaion Politeia*. Oxford.

Richardson, H. G., and G. O. Sayles. 1966. *Law and Legislation from Aethelbehrt to Magna Carta*. Edinburgh.

Roberts, Simon. 1979. *Order and Dispute: An Introduction to Legal Anthropology*. London.

Rogers, J. D. 1901. "Fragment of an Archaic Argive Inscription." *AJA* 5: 159–74.

Romer, F. E. 1982. "The *Aisymnēteia*: A Problem in Aristotle's Historical Method." *AJP* 103: 25–46.

Rosén, Haiim B. 1982. "Questions d'interprétation de textes juridiques grecs de la plus ancienne époque." In *Symposion 1977: Vorträge zur griechischen und hellenistischen Rechtsgeschichte*, ed. J. Modrzejewski and D. Liebs, 9–32. Cologne.

Roth, C. P. 1976. "The Kings and the Muses in Hesiod's *Theogony*." *TAPA* 106: 331–38.

Ruschenbusch, Eberhard. 1960. "*Phonos*: zum Recht Drakons und seiner Bedeutung für das Werden des athenischen Staates." *Historia* 9: 129–54.

———. 1966. *Solōnos Nomoi. Historia*, Einzelschriften 9. Wiesbaden.

———. 1968. *Untersuchungen zur Geschichte des athenischen Strafrechts*. Cologne.

———. 1982. "Der Ursprung des gerichtlichen Rechtsstreits bei den Griechen." In *Symposion 1977: Vorträge zur griechischen und helle-*

nistischen Rechtsgeschichte, ed. J. Modrzejewski and D. Liebs, 1–8. Cologne.

———. 1983. "Die Polis und das Recht." In *Symposion 1979: Vorträge zur griechischen und hellenistischen Rechtsgeschichte*, ed. Panayotis Dimakis, 305–26. Cologne.

Salmond, John W. 1913. *Jurisprudence*. 4th ed. London.

Sandys, J. E. 1912. *Aristotle's Constitution of Athens*. 2nd ed. London.

Schapera, Isaac. 1938. *A Handbook of Tswana Law and Custom*. London.

Schlaifer, Robert. 1943. "The Cult of Athena Pallenis (Athenaeus VI 234–35)." *HSCP* 54: 35–67.

Schlegel, Stuart A. 1970. *Tiruray Justice: Traditional Tiruray Law and Morality*. Berkeley and Los Angeles.

Seagle, William. 1937. "Primitive Law and Professor Malinowski." *American Anthropologist* n.s. 39: 275–90.

———. 1941. *The Quest for Law*. New York.

Sealey, Raphael. 1976. *A History of the Greek City States 700–338 B.C.* Berkeley and Los Angeles.

———. 1983. "The Athenian Courts for Homicide." *CP* 78: 275–96.

Shipp, G. P. 1978. *Nomos 'Law'*. Australian Academy of the Humanities Monograph 4. Sydney.

Snodgrass, Anthony M. 1971. *The Dark Age of Greece*. Edinburgh.

———. 1974. "An Historical Homeric Society?" *JHS* 94: 114–25.

———. 1980. *Archaic Greece: The Age of Experiment*. London.

Sokolowski, Franciszek. 1969. *Lois sacrées des cités grecques*. Paris.

Solmsen, Friedrich. 1954. "The 'Gift' of Speech in Homer and Hesiod." *TAPA* 85: 1–15.

Steinwenter, A. 1925. *Die Streitbeendigung durch Urteil, Schiedsspruch, und Vergleich nach griechischem Rechte*. Munich.

Stroud, Ronald S. 1968. *Drakon's Law on Homicide*. Berkeley and Los Angeles.

———. 1979. *The Axones and Kyrbeis of Drakon and Solon*. Berkeley and Los Angeles.

Szegedy-Maszak, Andrew. 1978. "Legends of the Greek Lawgivers." *GRBS* 19: 199–209.

Talamanca, Mario. 1979. "*Dikazein e krinein* nelle testimonanze greche più antiche." In *Symposion 1974: Vorträge zur griechischen und hellenistischen Rechtsgeschichte*, ed. A. Biscardi, 103–35. Cologne.

Thomas, C. G. 1977. "Literacy and the Codification of Law." *Studia et Documenta Historiae et Juris* 43: 455–58.

Thür, Gerhard. 1970. "Zum *dikazein* bei Homer." *ZSS* 87: 426–44.

———. 1984. "Hans Julius Wolff zum Gedenken." *ZSS* 101: 476–92.

Tsantsanoglou, K. 1972. "*Phonou Pheugein*." *Kernos* (Thessalonike): 170–79, 250.

Van Compernolle, René. 1981. "La législation aristocratique de Locres épi-zéphyrienne, dite législation de Zaleukos." *L'Antiquité Classique* 50: 759–69.

Van Effenterre, Henri. 1946. "Inscriptions archaïques crétoises." *BCH* 70: 588–606.

————. 1961. "Pierres inscrites de Dréros." *BCH* 85: 544–68.

————. 1983. "Le droit et la langue à propos du code de Gortyne." In *Symposion 1979: Vorträge zur griechischen und hellenistischen Rechtsgeschichte*, ed. Panayotis Dimakis, 115–28. Cologne.

Van Effenterre, Henri, and Micheline van Effenterre. 1985. "Nouvelles lois archaïques de Lyttos." *BCH* 109: 157–88.

Van Velsen, J. 1967. "The Extended-case Method and Situational Analysis." In *The Craft of Social Anthropology*, ed. A. L. Epstein, 129–49. London.

Vanderpool, Eugene, and W. P. Wallace. 1964. "The Sixth Century Laws from Eretria." *Hesperia* 33: 381–91.

Verdelis, N., M. Jameson, and J. Papachristodoulou. 1975. "Archaic Inscriptions from Tiryns." *Archaiologike Ephemeris* 1975: 150–205.

Verdenius, W. J. 1972. "Notes on the Proem of Hesiod's *Theogony*." *Mnemosyne* series 4, 25: 226–60.

Wallace, Paul W. 1974. "Hesiod and the Valley of the Muses." *GRBS* 15: 5–24.

Watson, Alan. 1985. *The Evolution of Law*. Baltimore.

West, M. L. 1963. Review of *The Oxyrhynchus Papyri*. Part 28, *Gnomon* 35: 752–59.

————. ed. 1966. Hesiod, *Theogony*. Oxford.

————. ed. 1978. Hesiod, *Works and Days*. Oxford.

————. 1985. *The Hesiodic Catalogue of Women: Its Nature, Structure, and Origins*. Oxford.

Whitelam, Keith W. 1979. *The Just King: Monarchical Judicial Authority in Ancient Israel*. Sheffield.

Willetts, R. W. 1955. *Aristocratic Society in Ancient Crete*. London.

————. 1967. *The Law Code of Gortyn*. Kadmos Supplement 1. Berlin.

————. 1974. "Cretan Law and Early Greek Society." In *Antichita cretesi: studi in onore di Doro Levi*. 2: 22–31. Catania.

————. 1982. "Cretan Laws and Society." In *CAH*. 2nd ed. 3.3: 234–48. Cambridge.

Wolff, H. J. 1946. "The Origin of Judicial Litigation among the Greeks." *Traditio* 4: 31–87.

————. 1975. "Greek Legal History: Its Functions and Potentialities." *Washington University Law Quarterly*: 395–408.

————. 1980. "Vorgeschichte und Entstehung des Rechtsbegriffs im frühen Griechentum." In *Entstehung und Wandel rechtlicher Traditionen*, ed. Wolfgang Fikentscher, 557–79. Munich.

SUBJECT INDEX

INDEX LOCORUM

Designer: Barbara Llewellyn
Compositor: G & S Typesetters, Inc.
Text: 10/12 Sabon
Display: Columna Open
Printer: Braun-Brumfield, Inc.
Binder: Braun-Brumfield, Inc.